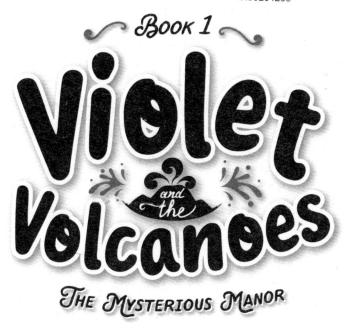

~ BOOK 1 ~

Violet and the Volcanoes

THE MYSTERIOUS MANOR

Written by

AMY DRORBAUGH

Illustrated by

BRANDON DORMAN

Contents

Chapter 1

Violet was exhausted. It had been over twenty hours since her family had left Ecuador, but it felt more like a week than just one day. Sleepily, she leaned her head back against the car seat and struggled to keep her tired eyes open. The ocean lay off to her right as they drove south toward the bottom of the island.

"I always forget how beautiful Hawai'i is until—" A huge yawn interrupted her mom's statement. "Sorry—until we are back here. It's a good thing the volcanoes are so active: we always have a reason to return."

Violet's dad nodded in agreement from the driver's seat. "Hawai'i is beautiful, but I would choose volcanoes in Alaska over Hawai'i any day. I prefer the snow to the humidity." Although the air conditioning in the rental car was on full blast, he made a show of wiping imaginary sweat off his forehead.

The best thing about Hawai'i, Violet thought privately, *is that it's an island, so we can't be very far from our rental house.* Despite her best efforts, her eyes drifted shut of their own accord. She jolted awake again when the car hit another bump.

"We're almost there, honey." Her mom studied her in the rearview mirror, and Violet saw her own exhaustion reflected in her mom's eyes. James and Emily Thatcher were world-renowned volcanologists, and they spent the majority of their time flying from one volcano to another. Emily was afraid of flying, which was unfortunate considering how often the family had to do it.

Stifling a yawn, Violet asked, "Are we staying in the same place as last time?"

"No," her dad answered. "The company is renting a new house closer to the volcanoes."

"Is it by the beach?" Violet asked hopefully.

"Well, nothing here is too far away from the beach, right?" her dad replied with a chuckle.

Out her window Violet caught sight of an old lava flow. The river of black rock was evidence of a past eruption of Kīlauea, the volcano her parents were here to study. Most of the leeward, or west, side of the Big Island was hot, dry, and covered in old lava flows. The windward side, on the east, was wetter and—at least to Violet—much prettier with its tropical rainforests.

Suddenly, the car slowed, and Violet swayed tiredly as they turned onto a small dirt road. James navigated around a large hole, the tires of their car going up on the shoulder. "I think we're almost there—"

His voice trailed off as they caught a glimpse of their home for the next twelve weeks. The car slowed to a stop.

"Well," Emily observed weakly, "it looks very . . . large."

"Yes, very large. And very—"James searched for something to say.

"Creepy? Odd? Dilapidated?"Violet suggested helpfully.

Perched on a small hill, the strange house was tall and narrow, coming to a sharp point at the top. Its sloping eaves, extravagant woodwork, and intricate balconies reminded Violet of the gingerbread houses they made at Christmas. Perhaps the house had been charming when it was first built, but the passage of time had not been kind.

"It doesn't look very Hawaiian, does it?"Violet said, leaning forward between her parents' seats. "It looks like it came straight out of a Charles Dickens book. Can't you just picture Mr. Scrooge inside, sitting alone in the dark, eating his bit of beef?"

"There must be some sort of story behind it," Emily agreed. "Who would build a house like this between a tropical rainforest and a volcano?"

What sort of story would I write about this curious house? Violet wondered. *Would it be dark, mysterious, and full of intrigue? Or more whimsical?* Immediately, she had the urge to sketch the house and tried to remember where her journal was in the mass of luggage.

Once the car was parked, Violet opened her door and climbed out, holding on to the frame as a rush of dizziness made her feel lightheaded. *Hopefully, the beds are in better shape than the outside of the house*, she thought.

Closer inspection did not improve the house much. The white paint had chipped away in most places, leaving the

entire house an unpleasant grayish-brown color. Shutters were broken and hanging at crazy angles or missing completely. Spiderwebs adorned every corner that Violet could see, and the entire house seemed to sag to the left.

"It might be a little odd, but it's a survivor. Look at that," James pointed out. Violet followed his gaze to the side of the house, where black lava rock from a previous eruption came within twenty feet of the house.

Slowly the three moved toward the house, but they all paused at the elaborate front door. A large "K" was detailed in lead and stained glass above an immense bronze knocker. No one moved to open the door, and Violet wondered if her parents were feeling the same sense of hesitation that she was.

"Well, let's check it out," her dad announced, hitching a bag onto his shoulder. "They said the door would be unlocked." He grasped the large door handle and turned it.

The door swung open silently, although Violet had been half expecting it to creak. They peered through the dim and dusty interior until Violet's dad flipped on the light switch, and an elaborate crystal chandelier above them flickered reluctantly to life. They were standing in a large foyer, luxuriously decorated in a style at least a hundred years out of date. Doorways opened to the left and right, and straight ahead, a grand staircase curved up to the second floor.

"Wow." Violet's exclamation, though soft, sounded too loud in the still room. Stepping into the house felt like stepping back in time.

"'Wow' is right," James replied.

Violet stared around her in wonder as they explored the rooms on the bottom floor. First, a narrow dining room with a long table and eight heavy chairs, where Violet could picture elegant meals being served on delicate china plates. Continuing on, they found a living room with overstuffed couches upholstered in rich velvet fabrics and an ornate fireplace. A tiny kitchen tucked in the back of the house behind the staircase completed their tour of the main floor.

Although the materials and possessions in each room were clearly expensive, the touch of time could be felt heavily in the house. Velvet pillows were worn thin, carpets were faded and fraying at the edges, the wooden floors bore deep scratches, and a thick layer of dust lay over everything.

"This house must have been empty for years, but it feels like—" Violet struggled to find the words. She had stayed in *many* hotels and rental houses, and they all had a similar temporary feeling to them—houses and rooms that were used but never *lived in*. This house actually felt like a home. There were books on the shelves and artwork on the walls. An umbrella stand by the door held three battered umbrellas. A hand-knit afghan was thrown over the arm of the couch. Violet almost expected to see a pair of shoes by the back door or a pot of tea steaming on the antique stove in the kitchen. "—like someone is going to walk in at any moment," she finished.

"Yeah," Emily agreed, gently touching an embellished gold-plated clock.

Cautiously, Violet reached out to pick up a blue marble egg from a low table next to the staircase. It wouldn't move;

it stuck firmly to the gold base it sat on. Violet frowned and changed her grip on the egg, rubbing the dust off its slick surface. To her surprise, the egg twisted easily in her hand, rotating on its base in a complete circle. A loud clicking noise came from behind her.

"Whoa!" she exclaimed as the wall behind her started to move. The three Thatchers watched, open-mouthed, as a section of the wood paneling swung outward several inches.

"What did you do?" Emily exclaimed.

"I don't know!" Violet stammered. "I just twisted that egg."

James reached out and pulled on the panel. It swung open. A smile lit his tired face. "I think you discovered a secret passageway."

"Like in a book?" Violet asked excitedly, leaning forward to peer inside. "This is the coolest house ever! Where does it go?"

James pulled out his phone and turned on the flashlight. The light revealed a narrow passage, about ten paces long, ending at a rough door with a small doorknob. Moving into the passageway with Violet on his heels, James immediately sneezed violently as their footsteps stirred up a thick layer of dust. They walked softly toward the far door and grasped the knob. It resisted turning at first but finally gave way, and the door swung outward.

"Where does it lead to?" Emily called after them.

Violet followed her dad out through another section of wood paneling and looked around.

"We're in the dining room!" she called out, and seconds

later, her mom followed them through. "How cool is this? Do you think there are more secret passages?"

"I'd say it's possible, pumpkin." Emily ruffled Violet's hair, trying to suppress an enormous yawn.

James shrugged. "It's a mystery . . . but not one we are going to solve today. I don't know about you girls, but I am exhausted. Shall we save the exploration for tomorrow and go find the bedrooms?" He carefully shut the door to the secret passageway. The three watched as the seams of the door disappeared completely into the paneled wall.

They returned to the foyer and closed the section of paneling, watching in fascination as the marble egg untwisted before clicking into place. Then the tired family climbed the grand staircase curving up to the second level of the house. At the top, four doors graced a long hallway. A glance into the first two rooms revealed bedrooms in the same formal, outdated style as the first floor. Her parents took the first room, decorated in rich blues and golds, but Violet continued down the hallway. The third door revealed a small but functional bathroom, and the fourth door opened to an office with floor-to-ceiling bookshelves. Violet closed that door again, with a promise to herself to explore it soon.

The hallway continued, and she came to a narrow staircase with a single wooden door at the top. *What other surprises does the mystery house have?* Violet thought whimsically as she climbed the stairs.

Her first reaction upon opening the door was simple pleasure. The small bedroom was tucked away under the eaves of the roof and was extremely plain compared to the rest of the house. Sloping down at sharp angles, the walls mirrored the peaked lines of the roof above, and the only place Violet could stand up straight was in the middle of the room. A simple iron bed frame was centered against the wall opposite a large round window that would flood the room with afternoon sunlight.

"Perfect," she sighed, letting her suitcase and backpack drop to the ground. The yellow blanket on the bed was dusty like everything else in the house, but when she pulled it back, the sheets beneath were clean and cool. Exhausted from her busy travel day, Violet fell onto the bed, which was as soft and comfortable as she could ask for. To her delight she discovered that she could see all the way to the ocean out her window. As she fell asleep, Violet wondered about the single light that she could see blinking somewhere out in the ocean.

Chapter 2

Violet awakened suddenly in complete darkness and groggily fumbled for the lamp. Checking her watch, she groaned. Four in the morning! Why was she awake?

Because it's nine o'clock in Ecuador, Violet thought ruefully. It might be the middle of the night in Hawai'i, but her body was still on Ecuador time, and it was definitely breakfast time there.

Still drowsy, Violet tossed back the blankets and rolled out of bed. The view out her window revealed nothing but darkness. *No, wait.* Violet squinted, trying to bring the blackness into focus and wondering if she was imagining that small twinkling light.

Is that the same light I saw yesterday?

Then her stomach growled, and she dismissed the light in favor of finding some breakfast.

Before opening her door, she paused with one hand on the doorknob. One section of the wall was clad in wood paneling with a fanciful border carved with tropical flowers. A glance around the room proved that the rest of the walls were bare and painted a plain white color. Only this small section was paneled.

"Hmmm," Violet mused out loud. "I wonder—"

She traced the largest flower with her hand, and one of the leaves seemed to move under her fingers. Obligingly Violet gave the leaf a firm push. It moved inward with a solid click, and the whole section of wood paneling popped open.

"Aha, gotcha!" Violet pulled the panel open and blinked in surprise. It wasn't another passageway after all.

It was a slide.

"*Who* built this house?" Violet exclaimed. Sitting down, she excitedly swung her legs over the edge of the slide. It curved out of sight, but Violet hesitated only a second before pushing off.

The slide was steeper than she expected, and she picked up speed quickly, turning in a tight circle. A thought made Violet nervous as she continued downward. *What if the person who built the house didn't complete the slide? What if the slide stops and I fall off the end?* Just when she was seriously considering panicking, the slide leveled out, and she slid safely to a stop.

Standing up slowly, Violet felt her way around in the darkness. Slightly to her left, light leaked around the edges of a door, and she carefully guided herself in that direction until she found a doorknob and gave it a firm twist.

Violet stepped into the brightly lit dining room. The slide had dumped her into the same secret passageway they had discovered yesterday! Her parents sat at the table, hands wrapped around steaming mugs, with tired eyes.

"Violet?" Her mom raised one eyebrow at her entrance.

"I found a new secret passage!" she told them. "A slide from my room all the way down here."

"You're obviously the first person to use it in a very long time." Emily gestured to Violet's clothes, now covered with dust and cobwebs. "I think we're going to need to do some cleaning."

Violet sat down at the table. "Couldn't sleep?"

James shook his head as he studied his laptop. "Nope. We're heading out to Kīlauea as soon as the sun comes up."

"Already?" Violet asked, grabbing a granola bar from a bag on the table.

"Pressure is increasing in the magma system, and no one is sure where the eruption will be," James told her. "Do you remember what happened in 2018?"

Violet nodded solemnly. "The crater collapsed, and magma escaped through a side vent, destroying a bunch of homes. Is that going to happen again?"

"I hope not." Emily shook her head. "But we don't know yet. What can you tell me about this particular volcano, Violet?"

As a lifelong homeschool student, Violet was used to these kinds of questions. Everything was a learning opportunity when your parents were your teachers and famous scientists. She swallowed her bite of granola bar. "Well, it's a shield volcano, which means it has gently sloping sides. Most experts consider Kīlauea one of the most active volcanoes in the world. And instead of one single place where it erupts, doesn't it have a whole bunch of craters?"

James nodded. "Two dozen of them, in fact."

"Right, and Kīlauea is located on the side of an even bigger volcano, Mauna Loa," Violet continued. "Ancient Hawaiians had a legend that Kīlauea was the home to Pele, the goddess of fire. They thought she lived in that crater with the really long name."

"The Halemaʻumaʻu crater." James grinned. "Very good, pumpkin. Extra credit for knowing the folklore, too."

"Dad and I are both going in today to figure out where they need us, but starting tomorrow, Dad will take the morning shift, and I'll take the afternoon so someone is here with you."

"Sounds good," Violet said. "What do you want me to do today? Should I start school?"

Emily shook her head. "Why don't you unpack?" She swiped one finger across the dirty surface of the table. "And maybe you can do some dusting?"

Violet giggled. "Can do! Can I explore a bit, too? I can see the ocean from my bedroom window."

"That's fine, but don't go too near the edge of the cliffs," Emily told her. "You're too curious for your own good sometimes."

"I won't!" Violet promised. "I just want to see if I can find the light."

"What light?" James asked absentmindedly.

"I could see a light from my window last night and this morning," Violet explained.

"That's strange," he replied, packing up his laptop. "There are no houses between us and the ocean. Was it a boat?"

"Maybe," Violet agreed and then changed the subject. "Do either of you know where my journal is?"

* * * * *

Two hours later, Violet waved goodbye to her parents as the sun peeked over the horizon. She unpacked her suitcases, put her clothes away, and carefully placed a large metal box on the dresser in her room. The box was securely locked with a small padlock, but she didn't bother opening it. After a lot of digging, she found her journal at the bottom of the last suitcase. The cover was emblazoned with the words "Violet and the Volcanoes—The Adventures of the Thatcher Family" and was more than half full of journal entries and sketches from the places she had been. Three days earlier she had written the last entry before they left Ecuador. Violet took some time to write about their current trip and drew some sketches of the strange house.

Then she spent the rest of the morning dusting. Cleaning proved more interesting than usual when pushing on a loose brick caused a secret compartment to pop open on the side of the fireplace. There was nothing inside but spiderwebs, but Violet smiled as she closed it, wondering what secrets it had hidden over the years.

In the hallway upstairs, she found herself studying a long line of family pictures. The first picture showed an elderly Hawaiian couple and their grown son standing in front of the mysterious house. The next showed the family, slightly younger, posed on a beach at sunset. Violet continued down the hall—and back in time—as the photos became black and white and the family grew younger and younger until the son was just a cherub-cheeked baby grinning at the camera. The last picture showed the young couple getting married, decked in layers and layers of flower necklaces.

Why would they leave these pictures? Violet wondered, touching the dusty frame.

By afternoon, Violet decided that she had done her duty and headed outside, stepping eagerly into the balmy Hawaiian sunshine. Behind the house she discovered remnants of a large garden overgrown with weeds, and—just beyond—the ground sloped gently toward the sea. Violet meandered this way and that, following a crooked path toward the beckoning ocean. There weren't many trees or plants growing in this area, though Violet could see a forest of flower-covered trees off to the east.

The sound of waves grew louder as she neared the cliffs. They weren't very tall here, maybe only ten feet, and the water came right up to the cliffs, with no beach below her. Violet stayed a careful distance from the edge as she explored.

Looking back at the house, she tried to calculate exactly where she had seen the mysterious light this morning. She craned her head to the right, where the cliffs were taller and curved inland and a large rock, shaped just like an elephant's head, jutted out over the ocean. Just beyond it a flash of bright color had Violet up on her tiptoes, trying to see. *Is it a boat?*

Violet stepped forward to get a better view. No, it wasn't a boat. It was a little house, more of a cottage, really, on a narrow strip of beach at the base of the cliffs. The color she had seen was the red roof, and a light shone from the back windows, even though it was the middle of the day.

Who would live in such an isolated spot? Violet leaned forward, trying to make sense of this strange sight.

She didn't realize how close to the edge she had come until it was too late. The sandy surface beneath her feet gave way with a loud groan.

Shrieking as the ground beneath her feet crumbled, she slid toward the edge in a shower of loose dirt and rocks. Violet threw her hands out, desperately searching for any possible handhold to stop her fall. Her hands scrabbled across the face of the cliff, encountering rocks, dirt, and plants, but they all ripped through her hands before she could grasp them. A searing pain pierced her right hand, and she cried out as gravity pulled her over the edge of the cliff.

Suddenly, she was falling through open air, her arms windmilling wildly as fear clenched an icy fist in her stomach. Violet had only a brief glance at the churning surf below her before she hit the water with a resounding splash.

Chapter 3

The impact drove the air out of Violet's lungs, and she plunged into the water. She kicked frantically, clawing at the water as she tried to find the surface. Her lungs burned, demanding oxygen. *Which way was up? Which way was down? Was she swimming in circles?* The terrifying need to breathe filled Violet with panic, making it difficult to think. She opened her eyes, but the salt water stung, and all she could see was darkness.

Finally, one hand broke the surface of the water, orienting her for the first time. Adrenaline gave Violet a burst of strength, and she propelled herself out of the water. Trying to gulp in as much air as possible, she dragged in a ragged breath, choking and coughing.

But her moment of relief was short-lived.

A wave hit Violet square in the face, forcing her under again and spinning her until she was dizzy. When she bobbed back to the surface, she saw that the waves were sweeping her back toward the cliffs. Violet started swimming. Arm over arm, she stroked away from the cliffs.

Once past the breaking waves, she paused, bobbing up and down on the swells. Searching the coast to the left and the right, her heart sank. All she could see in either direction were the steep cliffs. Which way should she go? She couldn't swim forever! Already her legs were tired, and the weight of her clothes and sneakers dragged her downward.

Violet became aware of a stinging pain in her right hand. A deep gash crossed the palm from her thumb to her pinky. Salt water burned in the wound, and red blood oozed into the water. She felt a shiver of fear run through her as she watched the curls of red blood disappear. *Couldn't sharks smell blood in the water? From miles away?* Violet tried to remember her marine biology unit. *Do sharks even live in the waters around Hawai'i?*

Angry at herself, Violet shook her head. She was wasting time thinking about sharks, getting more and more tired when she should be swimming! Shoving her hair back out of her eyes, she tried to decide which way to go. The little cottage she had seen from the top of the cliff popped into her head. *It had been on a thin strip of beach, hadn't it?* She could get out of the water there. But it was a long way away, and Violet wasn't sure she could swim that far.

What about the other direction? The cliffs curved away, and she couldn't see what lay beyond. She hadn't explored in that direction. What if there was a beach right around the curve? It would be much closer than the little cottage. But what if she swam all the way over and there was no beach for miles?

No, Violet decided firmly. It would be better to swim toward the known beach than to hope for one that might not be there. Before starting, Violet toed off her heavy, waterlogged sneakers and let them sink into the ocean. She gave a sigh of relief at losing the extra weight but watched them disappear with a little quiver of regret. They were her favorite pair of shoes.

The distinctive elephant-shaped rock in the distance made a good landmark for her to follow. The beach with the cottage had been just beyond that rock, so maybe it wasn't as far as she thought. With a determined breath, she started swimming.

Violet felt fairly confident as she glided through the water steadily, arm over arm, slicing smoothly through the ocean's surface. At her home in Arizona, she had spent a large part of her early life in the pool, making her a strong and confident swimmer. The salt water made her feel buoyant, and she swam quickly, paralleling the cliffs just out of range of the cresting waves.

But Violet had never been out in the ocean by herself before, and she tried not to think about what might be swimming in the water with her. To distract herself, she started counting her strokes.

One, two, three, four.

She slowed her breathing to match each arm stroke.

One, two, three, four.

She checked the elephant's head to make sure she was still on course.

Violet lost herself in the rhythm, trying to ignore the burning muscles in her arms and legs. When she felt like she couldn't swim anymore, she flipped over and floated, staring up at the cloudless sky. Although she promised herself just one minute, she counted to three hundred before she forced herself to turn over again.

"Oh no!" While she had been floating, the ocean current had pulled her back out. Now she had even farther to swim than before! Furious at herself, she angled back toward the shore, kicking angrily. But anger supported her for only so long. Soon her tired muscles slowed, and she fell back into her rhythm.

One, two, three, four. Breathe.

One, two, three, four. Elephant.

Did something touch her foot?

Violet spun in the water, peering downward. The sun bounced off the water, reflecting into her eyes. She couldn't see anything.

Soon Violet's world condensed to the exhausted struggle to keep moving. *Swim, kick, breathe. Swim, kick, breathe.* There was a moment of panic when she checked for the elephant rock again and couldn't find it. Then she looked up and realized she was right underneath it. Treading water, she searched again for the little strip of beach.

There! There it was! The cliffs gave way to a sandy beach tucked back in a small cove, and the little cottage stood in the exact center of the tiny crescent of sand.

Violet struck out with a fierce longing to be on dry land again, but her tired legs responded sluggishly, and her arms felt too heavy to lift. Her progress was agonizingly slow, and she knew that she couldn't swim much longer. She felt weak and dizzy.

Finally, a large wave caught her and propelled her forward. With the last of her strength, Violet tried to direct her path, but the wave tossed her around, dragging her back and then thrusting her forward again. Her right leg hit the sandy bottom of the ocean floor, and the merciless waves dragged her over it, scraping her from knee to ankle. Crying out in pain, Violet swallowed a mouthful of salty water.

Another strong wave tossed her forward, and she used the last of her strength to drag herself onto the sandy beach. Violet collapsed in exhaustion, the left side of her face in the sand, sucking in air and sand in equal measure and coughing weakly. Seawater was lapping at her feet, and she knew she should crawl farther up the beach to be safe from the incoming tide. But she couldn't move, couldn't think, couldn't do anything but lie there in the sand. A wave of dizziness pulled Violet over the edge, and as her vision started to fade to black, she caught a glimpse of someone walking toward her across the sand.

* * * * *

Violet's first feeling upon waking was warmth. Snuggling under a blanket, she considered going back to sleep. She was so tired. And her hand hurt.

Her hand hurt.

Violet's eyes popped open. She found herself lying on a long couch, swathed in a hand-knit blanket in shades of blue. Struggling to push herself up, she grunted in pain as her right hand throbbed. Glancing down, she realized that it was now neatly bandaged.

She looked around curiously. Was she inside the cottage? The room was tidy and had very little in the way of furniture. The long couch, a small dining table with two chairs, and a row of filing cabinets were the only pieces of furniture in the room. A small fire blazed in a fireplace along one wall, filling the room with drowsy warmth, and two closed doors were spaced evenly along the back wall.

Every nook and cranny of the small room was filled with potted plants. Sitting on the floor, hanging from the ceiling, and spreading across the table were dozens of plants bringing the scent of earth and life.

Violet sat up slowly, painfully. Her T-shirt and shorts were damp, and another bandage was wound around her left calf. How long had she been asleep?

The door directly behind Violet creaked open. She turned her head to look, but no one was there.

"H-hello?" she called out hoarsely. Standing up stiffly, she clutched the heavy blanket in hands that were suddenly sweaty. The open doorway revealed an empty bedroom. "Who's there?"

Something brushed against Violet's ankle.

"Aaaagggghhhh!" she shrieked, jumping onto the couch. A glance down revealed a large and rather startled orange cat. Violet laughed shakily and collapsed back on the comfy cushions, her heart beating loudly in her ears.

"Hello. Did you open that door?" She scratched the cat's head, and it leaned into her touch agreeably, so she combed her fingers through its soft coat. The cat purred and arched its back under Violet's hand.

"Friendly, aren't you?" Violet laughed. "I hope your owner is friendly, too." She gave the cat a pat and stood up unsteadily, padding across the wood floor on bare feet. Hesitantly, she tried the second door. It was locked. Wandering over to the table, she softly stroked the bright red blossom of an exotic-looking plant. A stack of papers on the table caught Violet's eyes. The pages seemed to be covered with mathematical formulas. *Stranger and stranger.*

She walked to the front window and looked out at the ocean. A set of footprints led down to the water, and another set returned to the cottage. The cat followed her and sat on top of her feet. Violet smiled at the comforting weight.

A stern voice behind Violet startled her.

"So, you're finally awake, are you?"

Chapter 4

Violet spun around. An older Hawaiian woman stood in the doorway, surrounded by a strange bluish light. She had long silver hair braided into a crown on top of her head. A sturdy apron covered her clothes, and a smudge of dirt graced one cheek. The cat abandoned Violet and ran to the woman's side.

"I've never had anyone swim to my house before," the woman stated dryly as she hung up her apron. Pulling the door closed, she locked it securely with a key from her pocket. "Where did you come from, girl? I presume you didn't drop from the sky?"

"No, ma'am. I mean, yes, ma'am," Violet stuttered hoarsely.

The woman raised one eyebrow. "You must have a story to tell. Sit down, and I'll make us some tea. It sounds like your throat is paining you some."

Obediently, Violet sat down at the table. The cat padded along behind and reclaimed Violet's feet as its perch.

The woman filled a kettle and hung it on a hook over the fire, her movements economical and elegant. Did the

woman do all her cooking over the fire? Or was the real kitchen behind that locked door? Violet was bursting with questions.

The woman sat at the table and watched her expectantly.

Violet cleared her throat. "I was exploring the cliffs, but I got too close to the edge and fell into the ocean. I saw your little cottage from the top, so I started to swim in this direction. I barely made it to the beach."

The woman seemed surprised. "I assumed you fell out of a boat. Where are you staying? There aren't any houses for miles in either direction."

The teakettle shrieked, and the woman rose to retrieve it. She poured steaming hot water into two teacups and returned the teakettle to its hook. Violet accepted a cup, wrapping her cold hands around it gratefully.

"Actually," Violet told her, "there's a big house just above you. We're staying there."

The woman's eyes widened with shock, and she bobbled her cup, hissing when hot water splattered her wrist.

"You're staying at the manor house?" Her voice turned suddenly cold and unfriendly.

"I don't know what it's called," Violet stammered, confused. "It's a big house, three stories tall. Is that the manor house?"

"Yes. What did you say your name was?" the woman demanded.

"Violet Thatcher."

"Thatcher. Hmmm," the woman mused, lost in her own thoughts.

The silence dragged on until Violet couldn't stand it anymore. "We got there last night. Is it your house?"

"My house?" The woman seemed shocked and even angrier. "Why would you think that?"

Violet just shrugged.

"This is my house. Has been for almost fifty years," the woman answered darkly, scowling down at her cup of tea. Violet didn't know what to say, so she raised the teacup to her lips and took a sip.

"This is delicious!" she exclaimed. The woman looked up, and the angry lines of her face softened slightly.

"*Mahalo*, thank you; I make it from my own plants."

Violet looked around at all the plants. "Are you a botanist or something?"

"Or something." The woman's lips quirked. "You've had quite the adventure, Violet. What do I do with you now?"

"Can I call my parents?" Violet asked, suddenly realizing how late it had gotten. "They'll be so worried."

"I don't have a phone," the woman said shortly.

Violet stared at her in shock. "You . . . don't have a phone? At all?"

The woman smiled at the incredulity in Violet's voice. "Don't need one."

"Maybe I could email them?" Violet suggested. The woman shook her head before Violet finished. "You don't have a computer, either?"

"No."

Considering this strange development, Violet asked, "Is there a way to get back up the cliffs?"

"The only way in or out is by boat." The woman paused and then added dryly, "Or by swimming, apparently."

Violet suddenly felt exhausted. Her skin itched with dried salt and sand; her injured hand and leg ached. Her throat tightened as she tried not to cry.

"How do I get home?"

Still on top of her feet, the cat seemed to sense Violet's distress and purred reassuringly. The woman glanced down at the cat.

"Nalu is right," she said briskly. "Everything is going to be OK. I'm expecting a delivery of groceries from Mr. Pakakiko any time now. He can take you back in his boat." She patted Violet's hand awkwardly.

The cat suddenly jumped onto the table and butted the woman with its head. She smiled ruefully at the animal and scratched it between the ears.

"You're right, Nalu," the woman told the cat and then looked up at Violet. "I haven't had any guests in a very long time. I guess I should say *e komo mai*. Welcome."

"Thank you, Miss—" Violet paused.

She hesitated briefly. "You can call me Miss Lilo."

"Miss Lilo," Violet responded with a smile. "Thank you for helping me."

Miss Lilo shrugged her shoulders. "It's a good thing you're so small, or I wouldn't have been able to carry you. Nalu is a good foot warmer, but he's not much help in an emergency."

The cat sniffed softly, jumped off the table, and stalked away.

"It almost seems like he understands what you're saying," Violet laughed.

"He's been my only companion for a long time," Miss Lilo said with a sigh, "but he's not much of a conversationalist."

"Do you live here all by yourself?"

"Yes." The woman's answer was brusque.

"But—why?" Violet asked hesitantly.

The woman looked around the small room. Her eyes rested on the locked doorway, and Violet noticed her patting the key in her pocket. Then she reached out and fingered the wide leaf of the same potted plant Violet had admired earlier.

"Plants make better friends than people," she replied curtly.

Before Violet could respond, Nalu ran to the front door.

"Well, my dear," Miss Lilo said, rising from the table. "It seems your ride is here."

Violet followed her out the door and down to a small dock.

Mr. Pakakiko was a jolly man with tanned, weathered skin and a thick patch of black hair tucked under a ball cap. He stopped his little boat confidently, but his eyebrows shot into his hairline when he saw Violet standing there.

"Well, well," he said as he tied the boat to the dock. "And who might this *keiki* be?"

"This is Violet Thatcher," Miss Lilo told him. "She had a mishap up on the cliffs and found her way to my beach. Could you give her a ride home?"

"'*Ae*, '*ae*, of course I can. Plenty of room once I unload."

Mr. Pakakiko matched actions to words and started unloading bags from the boat to the dock. "Where are you staying, Violet?"

"My family is renting the manor house," Violet told him.

He dropped a bag in surprise, and a can of cat food rolled out and down the dock. "The manor house? But it's been empty for years!"

"We are living in it for a while. I was on the cliffs up there, but I fell in. Miss Lilo took care of me."

The man shot an odd look at Violet. "Miss *Lilo?*"

Mr. Pakakiko hesitated over the name, the same way that Miss Lilo had when she introduced herself, but he recovered quickly.

"Well, I bet your parents are worried. Let's get this done and be on our way."

Unloading went quickly with all three of them working together. Mr. Pakakiko helped Violet down into the small boat, and she turned to Miss Lilo.

"Thank you so much for all of your help! Can I come back and visit you again?"

Hesitating, Miss Lilo looked down at Nalu, who purred loudly. "I guess that would be fine, if you really want to. Just don't jump off any more cliffs, OK?"

Violet laughed and sat down as Mr. Pakakiko started the engine. As the boat began to move away from the dock, Miss Lilo called out to Violet.

"Be careful, Violet. That house has secrets that are best left undiscovered." With that, she turned and walked back to the cottage, Nalu strolling behind.

Violet pondered Miss Lilo's words as the little boat skimmed and bounced across the waves. *What secrets? The secret passages? Or is there a bigger secret inside that odd house? Maybe the secret of why it has been empty for so long?*

Before long they passed the cliffs, and Mr. Pakakiko angled the boat toward a tiny jewel of a beach with a fat, stumpy palm tree growing out of a large black rock. There was no dock here, so Mr. Pakakiko slowed the boat until they gently bumped against the bottom. Then he jumped into the water and pulled the boat to shore.

"The manor house is just up that path there." He indicated a narrow trail curving through the trees. "It's only a ten-minute walk or so. If you prefer, I can take you back to town with me and then drive you home, but it will take another hour."

"No, this is great," Violet told him, jumping out of the boat into knee-deep water. "I'd rather get home as soon as possible. Mr. Pakakiko?"

"*Ae*, Miss?"

"Do you know why Miss Lilo lives all alone out there?"

Mr. Pakakiko whistled through his front teeth. "Can't rightly say I do. She's a woman who values her privacy."

"How often do you deliver to her house?"

"Oh, twice a week, usually on Tuesdays and Fridays."

"Could I get a ride with you sometime to visit her again?" Violet asked.

"*Ae*, Violet. You surely can."

Mr. Pakakiko pushed the boat off and jumped back in with the fluid grace of those who spend their lives on the sea. As he headed east, she waved before turning and making her way across the beach.

Halfway across the sandy beach, something crunched under her bare feet. A sticky liquid squished unpleasantly between her toes.

"Ewww!" Looking down, a slimy substance coated her foot and a broken eggshell lay half buried in the sand. Violet dropped to her knees and brushed the sand away from the shell pieces. The egg was much smaller than a chicken egg, and rounder, too. Digging deeper, she quickly discovered the rest of the nest just inches below the surface. Hundreds of eggs were piled into a deep hole. To her dismay, Violet could see that she had broken not one but three eggs.

She felt terrible for her clumsiness, but she didn't know what to do except to rebury the nest as best she could before starting for the path again.

The trail climbed steadily upward, and Violet realized how tired she was. What a day it had been! The sun was setting behind her as she reached the top and trudged toward the manor house and her worried parents.

Chapter 5

Explaining her adventure to her parents took several hours and even more apologies. After the initial panic faded, both her parents were fascinated by the story of the woman who lived alone in a cottage by the sea with only an orange cat named Nalu for company.

"I can visit her again, can't I?" Violet asked hopefully. Her parents exchanged a look over the top of her head, and Violet hurried on. "She seemed lonely to me."

"I'd like to meet her myself," Emily admitted. "She must have a fascinating life story. All right, you can visit her again as long as you get all your schoolwork done. I'll need to meet Mr. Pakakiko first and make sure he doesn't mind."

"And we'll need to keep an eye on the weather," James added.

"Why?"

"Apparently there's a hurricane forming out in the Pacific," Emily explained. "It's supposed to pass well south of the island, but you never know. Hurricanes can be unpredictable."

James grinned and ruffled Violet's hair. "Almost as unpredictable as volcanoes. Hurricanes almost never hit Hawai'i, thanks to the eastern trade winds, so don't worry."

Violet was sent to bed early that night, which she didn't mind because she was exhausted. Of course, she was also grounded to the house for the next three days, which she did mind, but she accepted her fate gracefully and used the time to catch up on her schoolwork. In the morning she worked on language arts and math with her mom, and in the afternoon she did science and history with her dad. In between school assignments, Violet searched the living room, dining room, and kitchen thoroughly, looking for the secrets Miss Lilo had hinted at. But all she found were dirt and cobwebs that she had missed in her first cleaning of the house.

On the fourth day after her adventure and her first day of freedom, Violet woke up with big plans. Her dad had assigned her an essay on animals native to Hawai'i, and she planned to head to the library in town to research sea turtles. After a late breakfast, she spent the rest of the morning doing chores with her mom. Then, loading her journal and a water bottle into her backpack, she headed out the door with her mom for the short walk to town.

The small town was nestled into the tropical rainforest that covered the windward side of the island. It wasn't raining at the moment, but Emily and Violet both wore raincoats just in case. The trees dripped water constantly, even when it wasn't raining, and the early afternoon air was muggy but not uncomfortable.

It was not difficult to locate the small library among the few shops and buildings. Violet gave a cheerful nod to the librarian at the front desk as they entered. Soon her mom was working busily on her laptop, and Violet was ensconced at a table in the corner with a pile of books. Time passed quickly as she took notes and drew in her journal.

"Did you draw that?"

Violet looked up. A Hawaiian girl stood next to her table. "What?"

The girl indicated a sketch of a sea turtle in Violet's journal. "Did you draw that yourself? It's great!"

Violet blushed. "Yeah. Thanks."

The girl plopped down in the seat across from Violet and pushed her thick braid back over her shoulder. "I'm Alula Manu. What's your name?"

"Violet Thatcher."

"Oh, you're named after a plant, too! We have that in common. I've never seen you before. How old are you?"

"Twelve."

"I'm thirteen! Are you a tourist? Can I look at your sketchbook? Please?" Alula reached a hand out. "You can say no if you want. My mom always says I'm as curious as a whole herd of cats."

Amused, Violet handed over her journal to the bubbly girl. "My mom says that, too. I'm not a tourist. My parents are here to study the volcano for a few weeks. They're scientists."

"That's cool. Oh, look at this one!" Alula flipped to a sketch of a young boy and a small dog.

"That's my friend Pablo. He lives in Ecuador."

"Ecuador! Wow, I've never been anywhere but here. Oh, and you write!" Alula exclaimed. "I'm a writer, too. Well, a journalist—at least I'm going to be, once I win the contest."

"Contest?" Violet asked, trying to keep up.

"The Walton-Blue International Writing Contest," Alula said proudly, whipping a flyer out of her pocket. "See, they have prizes for the best essay, the best poem—all kinds of writing projects! I'm going to win the prize for the best article. I just need to find a good story to report on."

Violet studied the creased flyer as Alula continued flipping through her journal. Her eye stopped on the listing for the best illustrated short story. The grand prize was one thousand dollars! *Maybe I should try writing a—*

"No way! No way!" Alula cried out, interrupting Violet's thought. She held up a page with several sketches of the manor house. "Are you staying at that creepy old house? No one has lived there for years!"

"We're renting it. But it's not creepy at all," Violet protested. "It's amazing and full of secrets."

"What kind of secrets?" Alula asked eagerly.

Violet found herself telling Alula about the house, the secret passages, and her fall off the cliffs. Halfway through the story Alula pulled out a small notepad from her back pocket and started taking notes.

"Keep going," she urged Violet. "This is a great story!"

So Violet told her about the tiny cottage, Miss Lilo and her fluffy cat, riding home in Mr. Pakakiko's boat, and the warning Miss Lilo had given her about the house.

"This is great! Like a story out of a book," Alula told her, writing frantically. "A mysterious house, a dangerous fall, a hidden cottage. You said her name was Lilo?"

"Miss Lilo," Violet corrected. It seemed disrespectful to refer to the woman as only Lilo. "She was nice, but she got really upset when I mentioned the manor house."

"Hmmm, that's interesting." Alula chewed on the end of her pencil. "We need to find out who owns the manor house and try to find the secret she was talking about."

"We?" Violet asked in surprise.

"This is the perfect story for the contest! You don't mind if I write about it, do you?" Alula asked, her pleading black eyes focused on Violet.

"I guess not." Violet shrugged.

"Good. The first thing we should do is go to the manor house and search for clues. Then I can do some digging around to see who the owner is. I'll go call my mom!" Alula walked to the front desk, leaving a bemused Violet to pack up and find her own mom.

As they walked, the girls collected the fragrant white plumeria blossoms that grew on trees all over the island. Each flower had five waxy petals tinged with yellow in the center and was the size of Violet's outstretched hand. Alula promised to show her how to use the blossoms to create a *lei*—a flower necklace. Alula asked dozens of questions as they walked, about Violet, her parents, and their travels. She asked Emily if she knew who owned the rental house.

"I'm not sure," admitted Emily with a shrug. "The

company we work for rented it from a property management company."

"Whoa," Alula said as the house came into view. "I've never been this close before."

"You ain't seen nothing yet!" Violet told her with a grin.

Inside, Emily left Violet to give Alula the tour and went to the dining room to work. Alula was properly awed by the house and amazed by the secret passageways, and she insisted on trying out the slide herself. She also immediately noticed the locked box on the dresser. Violet unlocked it, and they sat on the bed to look through it together.

"It's my home in a box," Violet explained. "Since we travel so much, it's where I keep my friends, family, and memories." She spread the pictures out on the bedspread, her hands lingering on one of herself and a boy laughing in a cave.

"Wow," Alula said, examining a blue origami swan and a small stuffed frog. "You've been to so many places!"

"Here." Violet handed her a photo. "This is Mount Fuji in Japan. Now that's a beautiful volcano."

"What's this one?" Alula pointed to another photo.

"Miravalles, in Costa Rica," Violet said promptly.

"And this one?"

Violet glanced at the picture. "Mount Saint Helens, in Washington."

"What's the tallest volcano in the world?" Alula asked.

Violet grinned. "Ojos del Salado, in Chile, on the border of Argentina."

Alula threw her hands in the air. "I give up! You're a volcano encyclopedia. I guess we should start searching."

"I've checked most of the first floor already," Violet told her as they went down the stairs. "I think we should start on the second floor."

Violet led Alula to the office. It was the first time she had been in this particular room since her family had arrived. The tall room was lined with bookshelves, all dusty, of course. Violet explored the desk in the center of the room while Alula investigated a bookshelf crammed with rocks, fossils, and other strange objects.

"Do you like homeschooling?" Alula asked as she picked up a bowl carved from polished wood. It was full of dried flower petals.

"Sure," Violet replied, sifting through a drawer full of papers. "Although it's really more like roadschooling since we're never at home."

Alula tried on a long necklace made of seashells. "Doesn't that get lonely?"

"Sometimes, I guess. But I love being with my parents." She grinned and shut the drawer. "And I get to meet lots of interesting people. Like you!"

Violet crossed the thick red rug to one of the bookshelves and started scanning through the titles.

"*Hawaiian Flowers*," she read out loud. "*Native Birds in the Hawaiian Islands. A History of Hawaiian Flora & Fauna.* Clearly, I didn't need to go to the library to research." Violet pulled a book, *Medicinal Plants of the Hawaiian Islands*, from the shelf and caressed the cracked leather cover, breathing in the musty scent of old paper. As she replaced the book on the shelf, she noticed small words carved into the front of the shelf.

Aʻohe hana nui ke aluʻia

"Alula!" Violet called out. "Look at this!"

Alula rushed over. "It's a clue!"

"Can you read Hawaiian?"

"A little." Alula squinted at the words. "I think this says, 'No task is too big when done together.' What does it mean? Do you think there's another secret passageway here?"

"Maybe." Violet traced a thin gap with her fingers. "Do you see this gap? It runs all the way around this center bookshelf. I think this bookshelf might swing out from the others, like a door. We just have to find the catch."

It was Alula who finally found it: a small lever on top of the bookshelf behind some decorative scrollwork. The bookshelf groaned. Dust billowed into the air as the left side moved outward slightly. Violet seized the edge and pulled as hard as she could, but her still-bandaged hand made it awkward. Alula stepped up next to Violet to help. Slowly the bookshelf started to move, revealing a dark passageway.

Alula dusted off her hands in satisfaction. "*Aʻohe hana nui ke aluʻia.* No task is too big when done together. It *was* a clue!"

A set of dusty stairs led upward into the dark.

Chapter 6

"What's up there?" whispered Alula.

"There's only one way to find out," Violet said. "Let's go."

"Hang on," said Alula. "I need to set every detail in my mind. Something like this: 'The heavy bookshelf creaked open slowly, resisting the intrusion into the secret it had protected for years. The smell of dust, old books, and passing time billowed out of the hidden passageway that revealed a narrow set of stairs.'"

"Not bad," Violet said. "I'd read that article."

Despite their rickety appearance, the stairs were solid under the girls' feet. The passage was eerily silent, and Violet realized she was holding her breath. She let out a shaky breath and then laughed when Alula did the same thing.

"It's a bit scary, isn't it?" Alula said with a sheepish grin.

At the top they discovered another door and a tiny slit window that let in a sliver of light. Standing on tiptoes, Violet peered out and caught a view of the driveway. "How do we get in here?" Alula asked. "There's no doorknob."

"Nothing is ever simple in this house," Violet replied. "Help me look for the secret catch."

The two girls ran their hands over every inch of the door and the frame. They pushed on the walls and stomped on every floorboard. Alula even boosted Violet up to check the ceiling. There was a brief moment of excitement when Violet found a wood knot in the wall that moved inward when she pushed it, but nothing happened—not even when Alula pushed it repeatedly.

"I give up!" Alula cried, rubbing her sore thumb. She gave the door a frustrated kick. "This is not good for my story." She held up her hands dramatically. "'Secret Passageway Leads Nowhere' is not a good headline."

"We'll figure it out," Violet reassured her. "Time for a break?"

"Yeah, I should go home." Alula headed back down the stairs. "I'll swing by the town hall and see if I can find out who owns this house. My aunt works there."

Violet followed her. "I'll keep working on the door."

"Perfect! If it's OK with your parents, we can meet up at my house tomorrow to exchange notes."

* * * * *

That night, dark clouds moved in, followed by a warm wind that whistled in the eaves of the old house. The next morning, James and Emily wore worried frowns as they watched the news. On the small TV, a bubbly woman in a pink dress reported on the hurricane, which was still on a course to pass south of the islands but growing stronger every day. Afterwards, she moved on to a story about the volcano and possible evacuations.

"Don't forget to work on your essay, Violet," James told her as he got ready to leave. "It's due in three days. We'll do history when I get home this afternoon." He gave them both kisses and left.

Violet and her mom spent the morning working together at the dining table, which was crowded with diagrams of Kīlauea and lists of sulfur levels and tiltmeter readings. Lunchtime passed, and James came home so Emily could head out to the volcano. After her history lesson on the Civil War, Violet and her dad spent some time trying to open the secret door. James agreed that the knothole had something to do with opening the door but couldn't figure out what.

Waiting for Alula to get home from school, Violet toyed around with some ideas for a story she could write for the contest, but she couldn't settle on anything she liked. Finally, she gave up, and she and her dad walked into town together, following the directions Alula had given her the day before.

"Violet! You came!" Alula waved from the porch of a house painted a bright and cheery yellow.

After speaking with Alula's mom, James told Violet, "I've got some errands to run. I'll be back to pick you up in a couple of hours." He headed toward the shops with a wave.

"I have so much to tell you, but first," Alula paused dramatically, "which country has the most volcanoes?"

Violet giggled. "Indonesia. At least, that's the country with the most active volcanoes."

"I'm going to stump you eventually," Alula vowed.

"Not unless you come up with some harder questions!"
Violet teased her.

"I'll work on it. In the meantime, I found out that the
manor house is owned by a woman named Leilani Aka.
She's owned it for six years."

"So it's not Miss Lilo," Violet said, disappointed. "She's
lived in the cottage for fifty years."

"Before that, it was owned by the Kahananui family. They
built it seventy years ago," Alula explained.

Violet shrugged. "Does that help us?"

"Knowledge always helps—eventually," Alula told her.
"I found a newspaper article about the manor house." She
whipped a copy of an old faded article out of her notebook
triumphantly and handed it to Violet.

"Wow!" Violet smoothed the paper on her knees and
read it out loud.

> *This week, Kekoa Kahananui, owner of Maui
> Macadamia Nut Co., broke ground on a house
> designed by none other than eccentric English
> architect Percival Hughes. Hughes, best known
> for designing grand houses in London and the
> occasional castle in Scotland, says that he
> is "honored to introduce traditional Victorian
> design to the Big Island." But British architec-
> ture won't be the only unusual thing about this
> house. Kahananui claims that "it won't easily
> divulge its secrets." One thing is for sure: we*

will all be watching the construction of this house with interest. Kahananui plans to live there with his wife, Akela, and his son, Makaio.

Violet looked up. "This is great!"

"I did an internet search, and the architect is famous for designing secret passageways in the houses he built!" Alula told her proudly.

"You are going to be a great reporter someday."

Alula waved off the compliment. "I'm just getting started. There are still a lot of questions, like why the house has been empty for years and who this Leilani Aka is."

"I think I need to go back and talk to Miss Lilo," Violet said thoughtfully.

"Why?" Alula asked. "We know she's not the one who owns the manor house."

"Yeah, but she knows something about it," Violet mused.

"Mr. Pakakiko will be down on the docks tomorrow; maybe he can give you a ride out there!" Alula jumped up.

The screen door squeaked open as Violet climbed to her feet. A large woman with a beautiful smile poked her head out of the house.

"*Aloha*, Violet! Alula has told us all about you." She turned to Alula. "Could you pick the boys up tonight? Kai is working, and Lono is out on the boat with Dad."

"Sure, no problem," Alula told her.

"*Mahalo*. Come back soon, Violet, and have dinner with us." She disappeared back inside with a slap of the screen door.

"It sounds like you have a lot of siblings?" Violet asked as they walked down toward the docks.

Alula laughed. "Four brothers. Kai is seventeen, Lono is fifteen, I'm thirteen, and Koa and Noa are five. My mom says they were the best surprise she's ever gotten."

Violet felt a small surge of jealousy. "My parents couldn't have kids, so they adopted me when I was little. I always wondered what it would be like to have a big family."

"It's pretty great, except when you need to use the bathroom in the morning," Alula joked. "Hey, there's my dad!"

A small boat with the words *Big Island Marine Rescue* painted on the side was pulling up to the dock.

"Marine Rescue?" Violet asked.

"Yup, my dad runs the Big Island Marine Rescue service. He also does search and rescue during storms and stuff. For people, not animals," Alula clarified as a tall man maneuvered the large boat in, throwing her a rope.

"Find anything today?" Alula called out.

"Nothing but a lot of empty sand." It was a teenage boy who answered. He nodded toward Violet. "*Aloha*, I'm Lono."

"Violet Thatcher."

"*Ae*, the girl staying at the manor house. Did ya open the secret door yet?" Lono asked with a friendly grin. His white teeth stood out brilliantly against his skin.

"Not yet. What were you looking for?"

Alula's dad answered, handing Lono a string of silvery fish. "We're looking for a sea turtle nest."

Violet felt an icy sensation in her stomach. "A sea turtle nest?"

"Not just any nest, Violet," Alula told her excitedly. "It's a *honuʻea* nest!"

"*Honuʻea?*" Violet asked.

Lono jumped in. "*Honuʻea* are Hawaiian hawksbill sea turtles."

Violet's mouth dropped open. "Hawksbill? Aren't they—"

"Endangered? Yeah, critically endangered," Alula clarified. "Hawksbill turtles are super rare. Some people think there are fewer than twenty nesting females left. One has been spotted in the waters nearby, and my dad has been put in charge of protecting the nest."

"First, we have to find it. We've searched all the beaches to the east," Alula's dad told them. "Every hawksbill is important to the population. We need to save as many as we can."

Violet looked at her feet, thinking about the nest she had tripped over. Was that a hawksbill's nest? Guilt washed through her, making her squirm. The thought of admitting to killing three endangered turtles, even accidentally, made her stomach sink.

"Have you tried searching the beaches to the west?" Violet inquired. Maybe they would find the nest on their own, and no one would have to know what she had done.

"There aren't very many beaches that way, mostly cliffs and lava flows," Lono told her. "It's more likely the nest is to the east."

"We may search to the west next week if we haven't found it by then," Alula's dad said. "Of course, now we need to keep an eye on the hurricane. The high tides from the storm could sweep the nest away. *Mauka* and *makai*, that's Hawai'i for you." He headed up the dock. Lono flashed the girls a *shaka*, shaking his hand with the thumb and pinky finger extended, and followed his dad.

"What was that your dad said?" Violet asked.

"*Mauka* and *makai*? It's Hawaiian for *mountain* and *ocean*. The volcano that way," Alula pointed toward the mountain behind them and then gestured out to sea, "and the hurricane that way."

"Hmmm," Violet hummed, distracted, as her guilty thoughts returned to the trampled nest.

"Are you OK?"

"Yeah, I guess. Alula? What happens if they don't find the nest? Will the eggs hatch on their own?" Violet asked hopefully.

"The eggs that survive will hatch, but a lot of nests get raided by wild animals. Even once they hatch, a lot of the turtles will get eaten before they make it back to the water." Alula led her down another long dock. Violet could see Mr. Pakakiko working at the very end.

Violet responded quietly, "So if they don't find the nest, most of the baby turtles will die?"

Alula nodded solemnly. "My dad says that only one turtle out of a thousand will survive to grow up."

"One in a *thousand?*"

Violet's thoughts raced unpleasantly. *They'll find the nest without me telling them, won't they?*

Chapter 7

Two days later, Violet crossed the little crescent beach silently in the early morning light. Her parents had dropped her off at the dock early so she could catch a ride with Mr. Pakakiko to Miss Lilo's cottage. Suddenly nervous, she paused in front of the door before knocking.

The door opened immediately, and Miss Lilo stood there with one eyebrow raised questioningly. Nalu darted through the door and ecstatically wound himself around Violet's ankles.

"I thought I heard a boat," Miss Lilo said, her face void of any emotion.

"Mr. Pakakiko is fishing today," Violet told her. "He said he would pick me back up this afternoon. Is that OK?"

"I guess it will have to be," Miss Lilo replied with a pointed glance at the boat disappearing in the distance. Nalu mewed loudly, and Miss Lilo pushed the door open farther. "Won't you come in?"

Violet followed her back to the table and took a seat, feeling awkward. Plopping down on her feet, Nalu purred

loudly, and Violet was glad that one of them was happy
to see her. Miss Lilo poured a cup of tea for Violet before
sitting down. She didn't say a word. Violet wondered if Miss
Lilo was as uncomfortable with conversation as she herself
was with silence.

"My parents sent you this." Violet broke the silence as
she pulled a white box out of her backpack. A sugary scent
suddenly filled the air.

"*Malasadas?*" Miss Lilo said eagerly, leaning forward and
sniffing.

Opening the box revealed a row of plump, round pastries.
"Baked this morning. Filled with guava, coconut, and my
favorite—*lilikoi!*"

"Passion fruit is my favorite, too," Miss Lilo said. "I
haven't had one of these for—for a very long time."

"Try one!" Violet urged.

Miss Lilo selected one of the doughnut-like pastries and
took a big bite, sugar crumbs clinging to her lips and hands.
Sighing with contentment, she closed her eyes.

"I feel like I'm twelve years old again, sitting on the
beach with my best friend after school. We would use our
pocket money to buy a *malasada* or a shave ice. I would
always get *lilikoi*, and he would get guava."

"Did you grow up here on the Big Island?" Violet asked.

"'*Ae*, I'm *kama'aina*."

"What?"

"Sorry, that means 'child of the land' in English. It's
what we call someone who lives here in Hawai'i. Actually,
I was born and raised right up there in the village." Miss

Lilo suddenly snapped her mouth shut, as if she had said too much. "Thank you, Violet. Thank your parents for me. I need to get to work now."

Miss Lilo's eyes flicked to the locked door.

"Can I help you?" Violet offered casually, trying not to show how excited she was by the idea of finding out what was behind that door.

"I suppose so. Come along."

Violet followed Miss Lilo as she unlocked the door, her heart beating quicker as another mystery was about to be revealed. Miss Lilo opened the door and strode through with no fanfare at all, but Violet stopped in total astonishment.

"Wow," she whispered.

The entire back of the cottage wasn't a cottage at all. It was a greenhouse.

The humid air smelled of freshly turned soil and flowers. Ten long tables ran the length of the long room, each covered with dozens of individual potted plants. Grow lights burned brightly above one of the tables, the light bouncing off the glass walls and ceiling. Miss Lilo tied on a battered apron and handed another one to Violet.

"Are these all the same type of plant?" Violet asked, walking down one row. Each pot contained a plant with thick, waxy green leaves and a profusion of small white flowers. "They smell amazing!"

"Yes." Miss Lilo picked up a clipboard hanging at the end of the table. "I call it an *ola* plant. That's not its scientific name, of course, but it seemed appropriate to me. *Ola* means 'life' in Hawaiian. This row is getting fertilizer with extra nitrogen today."

Each row of *ola* plants was set up slightly differently, with a clipboard at each end to record data, Violet noticed.

"You're running experiments with these plants, aren't you?"

"Why, yes," Miss Lilo replied. "How did you—"

"My parents are both scientists; they've taught me all about the scientific method. Are you a botanist?" Violet asked.

"A biologist," Miss Lilo corrected automatically and then bit her lip before hurrying on. "Why don't you start with this row? Give each plant a scoop from this bag and mix it gently into the soil."

They worked in comfortable silence for a while, moving from one table to another, consulting the clipboards and recording data from each row.

"You know, at one time this flower was thought to be extinct," Miss Lilo commented as they repotted a plant together. "Greedy people harvested it with no thought of the future. Now look at it! I'm discovering the best parameters to grow it so it can be preserved for future generations."

"That's amazing," Violet told her, wiping one dirty hand across her sweaty forehead. It was warm in the greenhouse.

"Plants are reliable," Miss Lilo continued. "If you take care of them and give them what they need, they will grow for you." Pausing for a moment, she carefully moved an *ola* plant to a larger pot and poured new soil in around the root ball. She spoke softly, with a glance at Violet. "I didn't think you would come back."

"I told you I would."

"In my experience, people never do what they say." Miss Lilo lifted the new bigger pot to the table. "I can't trust people. Not like I can trust my plants." She sounded bitter.

Violet was silent for a moment. "That's sad. I know there are bad people out there, but I think that most people are good people just trying to do their best, if you give them a chance."

Miss Lilo just grunted and moved on to the next table. This one was situated underneath the long grow lights next to a window. Violet realized something.

"Hey, this is the light I can see from my window! The light that led me to you!"

Miss Lilo looked startled, so she explained about seeing the light and following it down to the cliffs.

"You're staying in the attic room?" Miss Lilo asked slowly.

"Yes!" Violet watched her closely. "Did you know there's a secret passageway in that room? A slide?"

Emotions flashed across Miss Lilo's face, but all she said was "It's a strange house."

"Very strange," Violet agreed. "We found another secret passageway in the office. It's a stairway that leads to a secret door, but we can't figure out how to open it."

A small smile crossed Miss Lilo's lips. Violet once again felt that Miss Lilo knew more about the manor house than she let on. Suddenly, she wondered if she knew who Leilani Aka, the woman who owned the house, was.

"Did you ever live there?" Violet blurted out.

"What—no!" Her smile disappeared, and Miss Lilo dusted her hands off on her apron. "I think it's time for lunch."

When Violet followed her back into the main room, Nalu greeted their entrance with a flurry of meows. She stroked the fluffy cat while Miss Lilo assembled a simple lunch from food in her cupboards. They ate in silence. Violet wanted to say something but didn't know where to start. Finally, Miss Lilo took pity on her.

"Your parents don't mind you spending the whole day down here?"

Violet took the peace offering gratefully. "No, I think they're actually relieved. This way they can both go to work today."

"What kind of scientists are they?"

"Volcanologists," Violet said proudly. "We travel all over the world doing field research. Normally one of them stays home with me each morning to do schoolwork, but they're very busy with the possible eruption. That's why they're happy I've made friends."

"Friends?" Miss Lilo asked.

"Yeah, like you and Mr. Pakakiko and Alula."

"Alula?"

Violet told her about meeting Alula at the library and how the Hawaiian girl wanted to be a journalist and win the Walton-Blue International Writing Contest and how she was thinking about writing a story to enter as well. After lunch they returned to the greenhouse while Violet chattered on about the places she had been and the volcanoes they had visited. The afternoon flew by. Soon they packed away their tools and went out front to sit on the beach together, listening to the waves.

Studying the angry-looking clouds, Violet asked, "What will you do if the hurricane hits the island?"

Miss Lilo scoffed. "It won't."

"But what if it does?" Violet pressed.

"Don't worry." Miss Lilo patted her hand. "I asked Mr. Pakakiko to help me if I ever need to evacuate. Speaking of—" The sound of a motor floated over the water. "Time to go. I'm . . . I'm glad you came, Violet."

Violet waved at Miss Lilo and Nalu on the beach until she couldn't see them anymore. The boat ride back was choppy, the waves cresting in white caps across the open sea. Mr. Pakakiko dropped her back off at the beach with the fat palm tree, and as soon as he was out of sight, she turned and searched for the sea turtle's nest.

Unfortunately, it was easy to find. The sand on one side had been dug up, claw marks clear in the sand, and empty shells were scattered around.

"Oh no!" Violet exclaimed, dropping to her knees next to the nest. Maybe a dozen eggs or so had been smashed and eaten. It occurred to Violet that animals may have been able to find the nest because of the smell of the eggs that she herself had broken the last time she was here. So many turtles . . . gone. Sniffling back tears, she swept the sand away and was relieved to see that there were still many eggs, whole and unbroken. But how long would that last? Maybe she should tell Alula where the nest was, but that would

mean admitting to breaking the eggs in the first place. Violet cleaned up the nest as best she could, throwing the empty egg pieces into the bushes and reburying the whole eggs. With one last worried look, she hurried up the trail to her house.

Chapter 8

Alula was waiting on the front porch of the manor house, and she waved cheerily as Violet jogged the last few feet.

"Hey, have you been waiting long?" Violet asked.

"Nah, only about ten minutes," Alula said carelessly.

"I'm surprised my parents aren't back," Violet commented, flicking on lights in the gloomy house. "What did you do today?"

"Went with my dad to search for the *honuʻea* nest," Alula said, sweeping her braid over her shoulder. "He's beginning to wonder if it's too late; maybe all the eggs are gone already."

"Alula," Violet said slowly, her stomach churning sickly, "about that—"

Before Violet could say anything else, her dad rushed in, obviously excited about something.

"Violet?" James called out. "Oh, Violet, good, you're here! You'll never believe it! The seismicity increased this morning, and then the lava lake started draining rapidly, moving underground into the lower eastern rift areas. I need to find the maps. Where did I leave them?" He patted his pockets absently, as if the maps might be in there.

"Dad?" Violet prompted when he stopped talking. "What's happening?"

"What's happening! A fissure opened up in a brand-new location, and the lava is definitely mafic. Your mother is tracing its direction. The tectonic data is overwhelming! Now, the maps . . ." James started sorting through the piles of papers on the table.

Alula whispered out the side of her mouth, "Can you translate that?"

"The magma that's been building up at the crater disappeared today," Violet told her.

"That's a good thing, isn't it?"

Violet shook her head. "All that lava has to go somewhere. It's going to erupt from a new vent farther down the side of the volcano."

The color drained from Alula's face. "Like in 2018? When it destroyed all those buildings?"

Violet nodded solemnly.

"What was that about the lava?"

"The lava is mafic." Violet hesitated. "That means it's hot and runny lava, and it will travel fast. It can be very dangerous."

"I have to tell my family!" Alula cried, but Violet put a hand on her arm so that she didn't jump up and run out.

"Aha!" James, who had been unaware of their conversation, pulled out a pile of maps. "Here we go." Spreading the maps out, he marked the new vent with a large red X. Violet and Alula watched intently over his shoulder.

"You won't be in danger here at the house, pumpkin. The lava is running in this direction. It's closer to town than I would like." He traced a line to the southeast and circled the town with his finger.

"What about Miss Lilo, Dad?" Violet asked anxiously, but James was already shaking his head and pointing at the cove on the map.

"The fissure is below her cottage. She's perfectly safe."

Violet sighed in relief, noting how the lava was flowing between the manor house and the cove, but missing both. *Although, it's dangerously close to the—*

"Now, Violet, I have to go. Your mother and I will be late tonight. Will you be OK by yourself for a few hours?" James interrupted Violet's thoughts as he rolled the maps up briskly and tucked them into his bag.

"Can I go with Alula to warn her family?" Violet asked. Alula shot her a grateful look.

"That's a great idea. Stay on the main roads, OK? It will take the lava days to travel that far, and hopefully we'll find a way to divert it before then." James zipped up his bag and ran back out the door as suddenly as he had appeared.

"It's nice of you to come with me," Alula told Violet as they left the house.

"I need to talk to your dad," Violet said grimly.

They made record time from the manor house to town, jogging most of the way. It was obvious that news of the eruption had preceded them because a controlled chaos reigned among the houses. Adults rushed around, packing cars with valuables in case they needed to evacuate their homes, while children, some sniffling in fear, tried to stay out of the way.

"Alula! There you are!" Alula's dad waved her down. "Kīlauea is erupting again."

"I know; Violet's dad told us. It's heading toward us, but he says it will take a day or two to get here. Violet needs to talk to you."

He nodded, looking at Violet curiously. Violet took a deep breath to steady the butterflies in her stomach. Her legs were shaking, but she thought about the line of lava on the map her dad had shown her.

"Mr. Manu, I know where the hawksbill turtle nest is." Her voice quavered slightly as she spoke.

"You do? Why didn't you tell me?" Alula demanded.

Keeping her eyes down, she pressed on. "It's on a beach near the manor house."

"How do you know?" Mr. Manu asked curiously.

Shamefully, Violet whispered, "I accidentally stepped on the nest last week. I—I broke some of the eggs."

"It's OK, Violet." Mr. Manu's voice was gentle. "Accidents happen. After this volcano scare is over, we'll go and take a look at the nest."

"No," Violet shook her head. "That's the problem. My dad showed us a map, and the nest is in the path of the lava!"

Alula gasped, and Mr. Manu shook his head at this new information.

"Then there's no time to waste. Alula, go get your older brothers and tell them to bring the rescue gear," he ordered

briskly. Alula jumped up and ran off. "Violet, can you de-
scribe this beach to me?"

Faster than Violet thought possible, she was speeding
across the open sea in the Marine Rescue boat, seated
between Alula and Kai. The boat bounced violently across
the waves, but everyone held on tight and didn't complain.
They knew they were racing against time. Violet squinted at
the shore, looking for the distinctive palm tree that would
identify the tiny beach.

"There it is!" she yelled over the sound of the motor. Mr.
Manu nodded and slowed the boat slightly as he steered
toward the shore. When they were close enough, Kai and
Lono jumped into the water and towed the boat up the
sand. Violet led the group up the beach straight to the nest,
then stood to the side while the family jumped into action.

Mr. Manu carefully swept the sand from a section of the
nest and then, using a small tape measure he pulled from
his vest pocket, measured how deep the sand covering the
nest was. While he recorded the information on a small pad
of paper, the boys swept the sand clear to expose the whole
nest. Mr. Manu then measured the distance across the nest
and jotted down that measurement.

Alula produced a stack of empty egg cartons and a black
marker from their box of supplies. She carefully labeled the
box "Top Layer/Left Side," then handed the marker to her
dad. Picking up the first egg, he drew a small dot on top of
the shell and carefully set it in the egg carton, dot side up.
Kai and Lono were doing the same thing on the right side
of the nest.

Alula caught Violet's confused expression and explained, "Moving the nest is dangerous. Obviously not as dangerous as leaving it here, but still, it's easy to damage the eggs. Dad measured the nest so that we can create a new nest that has the exact same measurements as this one. We label the eggs so that we know where they were in the original nest. The eggs that are on the bottom of this nest will go on the bottom of the new nest."

"What about the dots you're drawing on the eggs?" Violet asked, handing Alula an empty egg carton as the first filled up.

"That's the side of the egg that was facing up in the nest. We'll make sure it faces up in the new nest, too," Alula said.

Mr. Manu carefully placed the full egg carton back in the box, while Alula labeled the new one. "Replicating the original nest gives the eggs their best chance of hatching well. Normally, we would never move a nest. We would just monitor it and protect it right here."

"But lava always wins." Kai grinned at Violet as he drew on another egg.

Violet watched closely as the four of them gently—but efficiently—packed up the entire nest, trying to help where she could.

"I count ninety-two eggs, Dad," Kai noted as the last eggs were packed, and Mr. Manu measured the depth of the empty nest.

He nodded in response. "That's what I got, too."

"How many eggs should there be?" Violet asked hesitantly, not sure if she wanted to know the answer.

"The average nest has 140 eggs," Mr. Manu told her.

Violet's heart sank. "So over fifty eggs were lost because of me? Because I didn't tell you where the nest was sooner?"

"No, Violet," said Mr. Manu kindly, "ninety-two eggs were *saved* because of you. Because you were brave enough to come forward."

Still upset, Violet took her seat in the boat. It was getting dark as Mr. Manu motored away from the little beach.

"Look!" Alula called, pointing back toward the shore. Everyone turned. Back to the west, in the distance, they could all see the bright glow of the lava flowing relentlessly toward the ocean.

"I'd say we got the turtles out of there just in the nick of time. Here comes the *pele*," Lono said as the boat picked up speed and headed back to town.

Lost in her thoughts, Violet was quiet for the ride. Back at the dock, the family unloaded the eggs, and the boys headed off to find a place to build the new nest.

Mr. Manu seemed to sense Violet's distress. He sat down next to her on the dock. "Don't let this eat at you, Violet. We all make mistakes. The important thing is what we do about them. You made the right choice when it mattered most. Now learn from it and let it go. Our past mistakes are only practice for the future."

"Thank you," Violet told him, feeling the tightness in her chest loosen just a little bit.

"Give me just a second to get the boys started, and I'll give you a ride home. It's too dark for you to walk, and I'd like to meet your parents."

"All right," Violet agreed. Then she had a thought. "Hey, Mr. Manu? Do you know the woman who lives in the beach cottage all by herself?"

"Sure," Mr. Manu said. "Leilani Aka. She's lived out there by herself for, oh, fifty years now. I'll be right back."

Violet looked at Alula, whose mouth had fallen open. She smacked a hand on her forehead in dismay. "It never occurred to me to interview my own dad! I did all of that research, and he knew the answer all along!" Alula moaned.

"So Miss Lilo isn't her real name," Violet said, bewildered. "And why does that name sound so familiar?"

"Because," Alula said dramatically, "Leilani Aka is the name of the woman who owns the manor house. *Miss Lilo* owns the manor house."

Chapter 9

Violet wanted to head back to Miss Lilo's cottage immediately. She still thought of her as Miss Lilo—not Leilani Aka—in her head. They needed answers. Why had Miss Lilo pretended that she didn't live at the manor house? Why had she used a false name?

But answers would have to wait. Mr. Pakakiko was too busy to sail out to the cove. Like everyone else in town, he was busy packing up his house in case they had to evacuate, but he promised to take her out in four days for his normal grocery run. Although she was impatient, Violet resigned herself to waiting. Her parents had given her permission to spend the days with Alula's family, which helped with the waiting. Violet knew her parents were relieved to have adults looking after her during the emergency.

Spending time with Alula's family was a new experience for Violet. There were so many of them, and they were so loud! Crammed around a large table for lunch, everyone was talking at once, laughing and joking. They teased each other constantly. After she had been there a couple of hours,

Violet found herself being teased, too, and she found that she liked it.

She spent most of the day on the beach with Alula, Kai, and Lono, digging the new turtle nest under the supervision of Mr. Manu. Carefully, they re-created the nest to the original dimensions and replaced each egg in the same approximate position. While they worked, they discussed the mystery of Miss Lilo.

"She's owned the house for six years?" Lono asked, placing another egg, dot side up.

"Yep," Alula confirmed, handing him another egg.

"But every time the topic came up, she got really angry," Violet told them. "She acted like she hated the house and everything to do with it."

"What I want to know is, why did she tell you the wrong name?" Lono asked. "Why would she lie about her name?"

"Hmmm." Kai rubbed his chin, scattering sand as he did. "Maybe she didn't lie. Maybe it's a nickname?"

A thought occurred to Violet. "Does 'lilo' mean anything in Hawaiian?"

"Yeah," Alula exclaimed, exchanging glances with her brothers. "It means 'lost.'"

"Lost," Violet repeated thoughtfully, "just like her cottage. Maybe she wants to be lost."

"No one *wants* to be lost," Alula protested. "Not really. Didn't you say she seemed happy that you came back?"

"She did." Violet shrugged, handing Kai the last egg.

"Maybe she's waiting for someone to find her," Alula suggested.

Violet covered the new nest with warm, soft sand and sent up a little prayer that the eggs hadn't been damaged by their adventure. The boys built a cage of chicken wire around the nest, and they marked it with warning tape.

"The only person who has the answers we need is Miss Lilo," Violet said. "But Mr. Pakakiko isn't going for three more days!"

"Hey," Alula said. "Kai could take you in our boat. He has his license!"

Kai shrugged when Violet looked at him hopefully. "Sure, if Dad doesn't mind. We could go tomorrow morning, if it's OK with your parents."

"I'll ask them tonight!" Violet promised.

* * * * *

"The general seismicity has subsided in the crater, and the magma pressure has dropped dramatically," James said, with a tired smile, handing Violet a sandwich.

"It doesn't look like there will be any other eruptions, and this one already seems to be decreasing." Emily dished some salad onto her plate. "Now, if the lava flow misses the town, it will be a good day's work. We should know by tomorrow afternoon whether we need to order evacuations or not."

"That's good news," Violet said absently, toying with her food.

"You seem distracted, pumpkin. Are you still worrying about the turtles?" Emily asked. "It was an accident, Violet. You know you would never purposefully hurt anything."

"No, it's not that. We got the nest reburied today. All we can do is wait." Violet lifted her sandwich but then set it back down. "Mom, why do people lie?"

Emily looked up. "That's a hard question to answer. Let me ask you something. Why didn't you tell anyone about the turtles right away?"

"I guess I was scared . . . and embarrassed."

"Exactly. Sometimes people lie when they're scared or when the truth feels too hard to face. But lying doesn't solve the problem; it just delays things. And it usually makes things worse in the end. Doesn't it?" Emily gave her daughter a gentle smile.

"Yeah." But Violet's thoughts weren't on turtle eggs. *What is Miss Lilo scared of?* "I want to go to Miss Lilo's cottage again tomorrow. Is that all right?"

"Is this just to get out of writing your essay?" James teased her.

"As a matter of fact, I finished that yesterday! I am now an expert on hawksbill sea turtles. I emailed it to you. And I finished my math for the whole week." Violet grinned a little smugly.

Emily laughed. "Well then, how could we say no?" She looked at her husband. "Is the weather going to be OK?"

"Should be OK tomorrow since the hurricane's still tracking south of the islands. Good thing—I can't imagine trying to deal with a volcanic eruption and a hurricane at the same time."

* * * * *

"Thanks, Kai," Violet said, jumping onto the dock in front of Miss Lilo's cottage. "Are you sure you're OK coming back for me later?"

"Do you really think I would just leave you out here?" Kai teased her. "I know you're a good swimmer, Vi, but even you can't swim that far! How does four o'clock sound?"

"Perfect! And tell Alula I'm sorry. I know she wanted to come along, but I think Miss Lilo will be more comfortable talking to just me." Violet paused, her stomach in knots. "If she'll even talk at all."

"Lulu will understand. She just hates to miss out on anything. You know how curious she is."

"Yeah, well, hopefully I'll have some answers for her soon." Violet took a deep breath, trying to drum up the courage to cross the beach.

"Alula actually gave me a message for you," Kai said, suddenly serious.

"Yeah?"

"Well, it's more of a question. She told me to ask you . . . how many volcanoes are on the Big Island?"

Violet burst out laughing. "Tell her she's going to have to try harder than that if she wants to stump me. There are five!"

Kai saluted her jauntily as he motored away. "*Aloha!*"

Still chuckling, Violet turned to face the cottage, grateful to Alula for helping to break the tension even in her absence. She crossed the beach, wondering if Miss Lilo would be angry after she learned why Violet was there. Steeling herself, she knocked on the door.

It took a few moments for Miss Lilo to answer, and when she did, Violet could tell she had been working in the greenhouse. Her apron was smeared with dirt, and she hadn't bothered to take off her gloves.

"Violet!" Miss Lilo exclaimed, a smile spreading across her face slowly, as if the muscles weren't used to the exercise. Nalu darted out the door and sat on Violet's feet in welcome. "I wasn't expecting you back until at least Tuesday."

"Alula's brother Kai gave me a ride out," Violet explained, patting Nalu on the head.

Miss Lilo tugged off her gloves and gestured awkwardly for Violet to come in. "I'm glad you came back. Would you like to come help with the plants? I'm adjusting the watering schedule on my *ola* plants. The newest breed of plants doesn't need as much water as the last."

Violet didn't move from her position in the doorway, and Miss Lilo stopped. "I would—I would like to help with the plants, Miss Lilo, but that's not why I'm here."

"Why are you here?"

"I have to ask you something." The words came rushing out. "I know that Miss Lilo isn't your real name, and I know that you own the manor house."

Miss Lilo looked stunned. Her mouth opened and closed, but no words came out.

Quietly Violet continued, "I just want to know why you lied about it."

"I never lied, Violet," Miss Lilo said with dignity, straightening up.

"But you said that you never lived in the manor house!" Violet protested.

"And I never did. It was my best friend Makaio Kahananui who lived there."

"Kahananui?" Violet repeated.

"I didn't lie to you, Violet, but I didn't tell you the whole truth either. Perhaps it's time the story was told. Would you please come inside and let me explain?"

Violet hesitated until Nalu mewed softly and butted her in the leg with his soft head. So she nodded and followed Miss Lilo into the cottage.

"Let me make some tea, and then I'll tell you everything."

Chapter 10

"I was born and raised in the village. I was seven when the Kahananui family built the manor house. It was a big deal at the time. I remember all the grown-ups talking about it, but I didn't really think about it at all until I met Makaio."

Setting a cup of tea in front of Violet, Miss Lilo sat down across from her. She cupped her own teacup in her hands but didn't drink.

"I loved to be outside. I drove my parents crazy by collecting every pretty rock or leaf or flower that I found. My favorite thing to do was to explore the forest behind our house. One time I got lost, and it was Makaio who found me wandering near the manor house. He's the one who gave me my nickname because I was lost. He called me—"

"Lilo," Violet spoke up. "Your nickname is Lilo."

"That's right." The older woman shook her head. "It used to drive me crazy. It was his way of reminding me that he rescued me. He took me back home with him, and that was the first time I was in the manor house. What a house.

It was a child's dream! Secret passageways, mystery doors, hidden compartments. Have you found the tunnel yet?"

Violet shook her head.

"It would take years to find all the secrets that house holds. Makaio and I spent a lot of time searching the house, but we were still discovering things years later. We were inseparable, best friends from the beginning. Lilo and Kaio. He loved to be outside as much as I did. We would roam all over the island, collecting pretty rocks, flowers, and leaves."

"That's why there are so many books about Hawaiian plants and animals in the office!" Violet exclaimed.

"Are those still there?" Miss Lilo asked, surprised. "Mr. Kahananui bought them when he saw how interested we were in the plants around the house."

"Haven't you been in the house since you bought it?" Violet asked.

Miss Lilo's voice hardened. "I didn't buy the house, and I haven't stepped foot in it for the last fifty years."

"But why? And how did you come to own it?" Violet persisted.

"Makaio and I went to college together, and we both majored in biology. We had a dream. Together we would work to protect and preserve native Hawaiian ecology. That was the plan, anyway." She took a sip of her tea, a scowl forming on her face.

"What happened?"

Turning, Miss Lilo looked at the open door leading to the greenhouse.

"Then the *ola* happened."

She stood up and wandered into the greenhouse, Violet trailing behind. Seemingly lost in thought, she meandered up and down the rows of blooming plants. When she started talking again, Violet got the feeling she was talking more to herself than to Violet.

"That was the beginning. The beginning of the end of our friendship. We were hiking together through an old over-grown lava field on the west side of the island when we came across a plant that neither of us recognized. It was a shy little plant, growing in the shade of much bigger ones. We took a sample back with us so we could identify it, but soon we realized that it was a brand-new plant, never before discovered."

"You guys discovered a plant?" Violet's eyes widened. "That's amazing."

"We thought so, too. We knew there was something special about it, so Kaio suggested that we experiment with the flowers to see if they had any medicinal qualities." She reached out and gently tugged one of the blossoms off of the nearest plant.

"Medicinal? Do you mean as in you can make medicine with it?"

"Yes." Miss Lilo brought the flower to her nose and inhaled deeply. "We discovered some healing properties in the oils and pollen of the flowers and developed a formula to harness that potential."

"That's good, isn't it?" Violet asked, confused by Miss Lilo's bleak tone of voice.

"It was supposed to be. Makaio was so excited. 'Our big break,' he called it." Her voice turned bitter. She crushed

the flower in her hand and let it drop to the ground. "He wanted to sell the formula to a pharmaceutical company. We would be rich and famous!"

"Wasn't he already rich?" Violet asked. "I mean, his family owned the manor house, and didn't his dad own a company or something?"

"That's correct, Maui Macadamia Nut Co. His dad built that company from nothing. He always wanted Makaio to take over. But Makaio wanted to step out of his dad's shadow. Mr. Kahananui was . . . eccentric, loud, and bigger than life. Makaio wanted to make his own mark on the world, to show that he could succeed, too. But I was worried. There were so few *ola* plants growing in the wild. I thought they needed protection."

More out of habit than anything, she picked up a watering can and started down the row. Violet stayed where she was, watching Miss Lilo lovingly tend to each plant.

"You would never know, Violet, from looking at this greenhouse that the *ola* plant was almost extinct at one time, would you?" Miss Lilo plucked off a dead leaf. "Because of Makaio."

"What did he do?" Violet ventured quietly.

"He needed to be famous, needed everyone to know about our discovery. He stole our formula and sold it to the highest bidder behind my back. The company came in and harvested every *ola* plant it could find. Pretty soon the plants were all gone. Makaio betrayed me and betrayed our dream of protecting Hawai'i. My best friend betrayed me." A tear rolled down Miss Lilo's cheek.

Violet waited a moment, but when Miss Lilo didn't continue, she burst out, "But that doesn't explain why you own the manor house, or why you live here."

Miss Lilo wiped the tear away, leaving a smudge of dirt under her right eye. Briskly now, she told Violet, "I never spoke to Makaio again. He tried to give me half of the money from the sale of the formula, but I didn't want it. I spent two years hiking across the island until I finally found it—one last *ola* plant. I knew I had to protect it, keep it safe, and bring it back to life. If the company that owns the formula knew about it, they would do anything to get their hands on it. I had to try and fix what Makaio had broken. My family was all gone by then; both of my parents had passed on. So I moved to this cottage and made it my life's work to nurture this plant and keep its existence a secret."

"So that's why you lock the door to your greenhouse?"

"I got into that habit when I first moved here. Just in case Makaio tried to come and get the last of the plants. I don't need to anymore, but there is comfort in routine. Look at this."

Leading the way to a large cupboard against the wall, Miss Lilo pulled it open. It was full of boxes, each containing stacks of small brown envelopes—thousands and thousands of envelopes. Miss Lilo picked one up and gestured for Violet to hold out her hand.

"Are these seeds?" Violet asked in wonder as Miss Lilo poured the contents into her hand.

"Yes. My life's work." She opened two more cupboards, each stuffed with boxes full of envelopes. "I've developed

twelve different varieties of *ola* plants over the years. I
wanted varieties that need less water or sunlight, that are
hardier or grow faster."

Violet studied the seeds in her hand. "But every *ola* plant
is here in the cottage, right? Shouldn't they be growing in
the wild again?"

"That was always the plan," Miss Lilo admitted, holding
up the envelope so Violet could pour the seeds back in. "To
wait until the pharmaceutical company forgot all about the
formula and then plant them across the island, in the lava
fields they love." She suddenly sounded tired. "But I think
that will be someone else's life's work. I've been in this
cottage for so long that I don't think I'll ever leave."

After taking off her apron, Miss Lilo ushered Violet into
the living room. She started to lock the door behind her,
but then laughed at herself and slid the key back into her
pocket, leaving the door unlocked. They sat down at the
table.

Violet noticed the *malasada* box still on the table from
her last visit. She gestured to it. "Do you have some left?"

Miss Lilo slid the box open. "I cut them all into pieces,
and I've been eating one each day. Trying to make them last.
Do you want one? They're a little stale."

"No, you eat them," Violet said, resolving to bring a fresh
box with her next time. "I still have one question."

"Why do I own the manor house?" Miss Lilo stared at
the pastry in her hand. "Makaio left the island soon after
he sold the formula. Traveling the world, his mom told me.
But ten years ago or so, Makaio started sending me letters.

I never opened any of them. I threw them all in the trash. After a couple of months, he stopped writing. I never heard from him again."

"Oh!" Violet exclaimed. "But what if he wanted to apologize?"

"Trust me, he didn't, not Kaio. Anyway, six years ago Mr. Pakakiko brought a letter from a fancy lawyer. Makaio had passed away, and in his will, he left me the manor house. He must have felt guilty."

"Or maybe he was sorry!" Violet protested.

Ignoring that, she continued, "I didn't want the house, of course. It's just been sitting there empty for years. I never even visited it."

"So that's why it's still full of stuff, all the Kahananuis' things and pictures," Violet whispered.

Miss Lilo sighed and then continued briskly, "Well, the truth of the matter is that saving a rare plant in a hidden cottage doesn't pay very well. I needed some money, so I decided to rent it out. I learned that my first customers would be a pair of scientists and their daughter coming here to study a volcano. The next thing I knew, you washed up on my beach."

Chapter 11

Violet was quiet on the boat ride home, a thousand thoughts in her head. As they pulled up to the dock, they found Alula waiting for them.

"Alula! I have so much to tell you!" Violet said as the boat stopped.

"I have so much to tell *you*," Alula responded, with an unusually serious expression.

That's when Violet noticed the strange bustle of activity at the docks and among the beach houses. Violet climbed out of the boat and seized Alula's arm.

"Is it the volcano? Is the lava headed for town? Do we need to evacuate? Are my parents OK?"

Alula patted Violet's hand, still wrapped around her own arm. "The lava flow shifted and is headed for the sea. It's not going to come anywhere close to us, although it did destroy the only road between here and the national park. Your parents called my dad a couple of minutes ago. The evacuation warnings for the eruption have been canceled. But they're stuck on the wrong side of the destroyed road. You're supposed to stay with my family until they figure out how to get home."

Violet heaved a sigh of relief.

"If the evacuation order has been lifted, then what's going on?" Kai asked, gesturing at all the frantic activity.

"That's what I've been trying to tell you guys. It's not the eruption we're worried about now. It's the hurricane."

"The hurricane!" Kai and Violet exclaimed in unison.

"Yeah, apparently it turned or shifted or something. It's heading straight for the island now, coming up from the south." Alula started back up the dock, and the others followed.

"How strong?" Kai asked.

"It's a Category 2 right now, but they expect it to strengthen in the next couple of hours. Likely a Category 3 when it makes landfall tomorrow around lunchtime. C'mon, Mom and Dad need our help."

"Is Category 3 bad?" Violet asked, panting as they jogged. She saw the surprised look on Kai's face and added defensively, "Hey, I know all about volcanoes, not hurricanes!"

"Category 3 means winds over one hundred miles an hour," Alula told her.

"Oh, good!" Mr. Manu exclaimed as they walked through the door. "You guys are home. Kai, help me cover the windows. Girls, run to the market and help Mom carry home the supplies."

They spent the rest of the day helping prepare the town for the impending storm. Everyone was covering windows and glass doors with sheets of plywood, tying down loose objects, and stocking up on water and food. The store shelves were empty by early evening as residents rushed to get supplies. After the Manu house was prepared, the family moved on to help others, especially the older residents who needed assistance.

"What about Miss Lilo?" Alula asked at one point during the day.

"Oh, it's OK," Violet told her. "She said that Mr. Paka-kiko would help her evacuate. Speaking of her—" But at that moment they were called to carry groceries, and they hurried to help.

The family gathered around the kitchen table late that evening, quietly eating bowls of soup and some fresh-cut pineapple in an exhausted silence.

"Do we need to evacuate?" Alula's mom asked her husband quietly. Little five-year-old Koa snored on her shoulder, and his twin was draped across Kai's lap.

"Possibly." Mr. Manu frowned. "The flooding could be bad. But where should we go? The west road was destroyed by the eruption."

"If only we had more warning, we could have gone to Aunt Lara's house in Kona," Alula spoke up, her voice drag-ging with fatigue.

"We need to get to higher ground," Lono added worriedly.

"What about the manor house?" Violet spoke up. Every-one looked at her in surprise. "It's up on the cliffs, above the flood zones. And it's huge! I bet most of the town could fit inside."

Everyone looked at Mr. Manu, who considered the idea. "It's just sitting there empty," Violet insisted.

Mr. Manu nodded thoughtfully. "That's brilliant, Violet. The manor house is perfect. Lono, Kai, run and tell everyone that we'll evacuate to the manor house at first light. Everyone else, get some sleep. Tomorrow will be a busy day."

As Violet snuggled into a sleeping bag on the floor in Alula's room, she realized that with the busy day, she had never gotten a chance to tell her friend what she had learned about Miss Lilo. Oh well, there was always tomorrow. Her last thoughts were of her parents, hoping they were warm and safe, wherever they were.

* * * * *

Violet spoke with her parents early the next morning. They were safe and holed up in a hotel for the time being. She promised to stay with Alula's family until they could get home again. The whole family was awake and driving up the hill before sunrise.

The first of the evacuees started arriving at the manor house just after dawn. Sheets of rain from the storm had reached the island, whipping here and there with the rising wind. Violet and Alula welcomed each family as they arrived, helping them find a place to wait out the storm, while Alula's parents helped evacuate anyone from town who couldn't drive, ferrying them up to the manor house.

It was Violet's idea to show the frightened children the slide, and soon a line of kids was moving from the attic room to the dining room and back again. Their delighted

laughter was a strange counterpoint to the worried whisper-
ings of the adults.

"That's the last of them," Mr. Manu said, coming through
the door with a gust of rain and wind. He shook the water
out of his eyes. "Everyone else evacuated to the east."

"Mama is in the kitchen," Alula told him, "making some
food for everyone."

"I'll just go see if she needs any help."

Violet and Alula sank down on the bottom step of the
stairs, one of the few places left to sit in the crowded house.
The kids continued to brush by them on their way up to the
slide.

"This is the worst part," Alula told her, propping her chin
up with her hand. "The waiting."

"Yeah," Violet agreed. "Hey, I never told you what I
learned from Miss Lilo." Alula pulled out her notebook
and started scribbling while Violet told her the whole
story.

"Wow," she said when Violet finished. "So she owns this
house but hasn't been here in fifty years?"

"Mmm-hmm," Violet hummed, distracted because she
had just caught a glimpse of someone in the living room. "Is
that Mr. Pakakiko?"

Not waiting for an answer, she jumped up and headed
straight for the man wearing a ball cap and sitting on the
couch in the living room. He saw her coming and smiled
broadly.

"Violet!" he exclaimed. "Thank you so much for letting
us use the manor house. I must admit, I've always wanted

to see the inside. This is my wife, Layla. Layla, this is the young girl I told you about."

Violet murmured a hello and then asked, "Mr. Pakakiko, did you already evacuate Miss Lilo? Is she here somewhere?" Violet scanned the room for the older woman.

Mr. Pakakiko looked confused. "Miss Lilo? No, she told me that she had made arrangements with a family member if she ever needed to evacuate."

"But—she doesn't have any family here," Violet protested. "She told me . . ." but her voice trailed off weakly. Mr. and Mrs. Pakakiko watched her with concern. "Excuse me, please."

Whispering urgently, Violet tugged Alula back into the foyer. "Miss Lilo isn't evacuating! We have to do something!"

"Maybe she asked someone else to help her," Alula said reasonably.

"No, she told me that Mr. Pakakiko would help her, and she told Mr. Pakakiko that someone else was helping her. Don't you see?" Violet said in frustration. "When I was there yesterday, she told me that she wouldn't leave that cottage of hers, and the hurricane is coming straight at her little beach!"

"All right, all right," Alula said, her forehead wrinkling with alarm. "What should we do?"

"We need to call search and rescue, right?" Violet asked.

Alula's eyes brightened. "That's my dad; he's with search and rescue!"

Violet seized Alula's arm again and dragged her through

the crowd in the dining room to the little kitchen. They took turns telling Alula's parents what was happening, interrupting each other in their haste to get the story out.

"We have to go rescue her!" Violet insisted.

Alula's parents exchanged concerned looks.

"Is there enough time?" her mother asked.

"The storm's still a long way from making landfall," Mr. Manu responded.

"But the wind is already so strong!"

"There's no one else close enough."

Violet listened to the exchange, her chest tight with fear. What if they said no?

Mrs. Manu sighed heavily. "You go, Kaleo. It's your duty, and I can't bear the thought of that old woman out there by herself in this storm. Hurry, and please come back safely."

Blowing his wife a kiss, he headed straight for the front door.

"Mr. Manu?" Violet ran after him. "I have to go with you." Seeing the immediate rejection in his face, she hurried on before he could say anything. "Miss Lilo knows me. She'll listen to me."

He hesitated for just a moment before agreeing. "Alula, you stay here. I'll take Kai with me; he's been trained in search-and-rescue procedures."

Alula opened her mouth to protest, but a single look from her father made her nod glumly and sit down.

"How am I supposed to win the Walton-Blue International Writing Contest if I keep missing all the good bits?" she complained to herself.

* * * * *

Driving to the docks seemed to take ages, even though Violet knew Mr. Manu was driving as fast as he safely could. The car screeched to a halt in front of the abandoned docks, and Kai and his dad burst into action, untying the boat, loading in extra safety gear, and getting it ready to go. Violet didn't argue about the time it took to put on the wet sea gear and a life preserver.

The sea was angry. It seemed to Violet as if it were alive, an immense monster determined to prevent their passage. She imagined hundreds of fluid arms rising from the ocean, desperate to stop the little boat as it raced through the storm. Driving wind and rain stung Violet's face, so she buried her face in her arms, bracing herself against the movement of the boat.

The boat began to slow, crashing straight into wave after wave as Mr. Manu pointed the bow toward the land. Squinting through the rain, Violet desperately tried to catch a glimpse of the cottage, but she couldn't see anything.

Kai yelled at his dad, "I think the dock is underwater."

"We're going to have to drive right up on the beach!" Mr. Manu shouted back. "Get ready to jump out and tow us in, Kai!"

Deftly, Mr. Manu aimed for the left side of the beach, trying to avoid the submerged dock. The bottom of the boat scraped against the sand, and Kai scurried overboard, grabbing the rope and pulling them more firmly up onto the beach. Mr. Manu killed the motor.

"I'll stay with the boat," he yelled, gesturing at Violet and Kai. "If it floats away, we'll be in a world of trouble. You two go and get her."

Violet instantly jumped over the edge of the boat, landing in water almost up to her knees, and headed to her right, trying to get her bearings. Normally, the little house sat just above the high-tide line, but the sea was much higher than usual. The strong winds pushed against Kai and Violet, slowing them down as they ran down the beach.

"There's the cottage!" Violet yelled as a dim shape appeared through the driving rain. "Oh no, Kai! Look!"

The storm surge had driven the ocean all the way up to the little house already. The cottage was flooding.

Chapter 12

Violet pushed the door to the cottage open as the waves swept over her feet and broke on the walls of the house, splattering her and Kai with salt water. With Kai following on her heels, she splashed inside.

"Miss Lilo?" Violet scanned the front room. Even in the dim light, she realized that the entire room was already flooded. Water sloshed around her ankles as she waded forward.

A grumpy and slightly panicked growling noise startled Violet. A pathetically wet Nalu was stranded on the back of the couch, much smaller than usual with all of his fluffy fur wetted down and sticking to his body. Mewing piteously, he paced up and down the length of the couch.

"Nalu!" Violet cried, sloshing over to him. "We're here to rescue you. Where is Miss Lilo?" The terrified cat licked her hand. She could tell that he was scared. "I'll be back for you, OK, boy?"

"Where do you think she is?" Kai asked. "In the bedroom? Or maybe she already left with someone else?"

"No." Violet shook her head in denial. "She would never leave Nalu. She has to be here."

"Well, we need to find her and get out." Kai lifted a soggy shoe. "The water is getting higher."

"She's probably in the greenhouse. Follow me."

Violet slogged toward the back of the cottage, water dragging at her feet with each step. It felt like she was moving through quicksand, like time was rushing forward and she couldn't keep up.

"Miss Lilo!" she yelled. "Where are you?"

"Violet!"

At the sound of the frantic voice, Violet surged forward into the greenhouse, but she couldn't see anyone in the large room.

"Miss Lilo?" she called again.

"Here! Quick, help me save them!"

Following the anxious voice to the far wall, they found Miss Lilo on her knees in front of the cupboards, desperately dumping the boxes of seeds into a large bag.

"Miss Lilo!" Violet fell to her knees next to her in the water. "We have to go! We're here to rescue you."

"I can't leave without my plants," Miss Lilo cried, grabbing another box and dumping the contents into her bag.

"We don't have time for this!" Kai yelled impatiently. "The water is rising." He grabbed Miss Lilo's arm and tried to pull her to her feet, but she jerked away and grabbed another box.

"Please, Violet, please! It's my life's work. I can't leave it here to be swept away into the sea." Miss Lilo looked up, tears streaming down her face, mingling with the spray of seawater.

Violet looked at Kai helplessly. "I don't think she'll leave unless we help her."

He frowned, looking at the water pouring through the door of the greenhouse. His face firmed up. "We can take one load to the boat, but we have to do it now."

"Thank you!" Miss Lilo cried. "I'll bring the seeds; you two grab as many plants as you can."

Violet ran down the nearest row of tables and started grabbing plants, tucking them under her arms and carrying as many as she could. Kai followed her, his longer arms holding twice as many plants. Miss Lilo dumped one more box of seed packets into her bag.

"That's it!" Kai yelled. "We have to go *now* if we're going to make it out!"

Miss Lilo gave an anguished look at her greenhouse and the hundreds of *ola* plants they were leaving behind. "Follow me," she cried, heading for the back of the greenhouse. The two kids followed as quickly as they could, burdened down by the heavy potted plants. Miss Lilo couldn't resist grabbing a couple plants as she slogged down the row toward a door at the back that Violet had never seen before. But when she tried to pull the door open, the water pushed against it, holding it shut.

"It's stuck!" she cried.

Thinking quickly, Kai picked up one of the potted plants. "Stand back!" he yelled. After waiting a moment, he threw the plant through the glass wall of the greenhouse. The glass pane shattered into a thousand pieces, raining down on Kai. Violet ducked her head, shielding her face in the leaves of the plants she was carrying.

"C'mon," Kai called, shaking the glass out of his hair and pushing through the hole in the wall. Ocean waves carried away the shattered glass, and Miss Lilo and Violet stepped gingerly through the hole.

Outside they could see that only a small strip of sand remained at the base of the cliffs. They made better time running on the wet sand. Kai led them toward the boat, and soon they saw Mr. Manu gesturing at them to hurry.

"Quick, we need to get out of here!" he yelled over the raging storm. Kai reached the boat first and started lobbing his plants to his father, who dropped them in the bottom of the boat. Turning back around, he grabbed Miss Lilo's bag and helped her into the boat.

Later, Violet was never sure if she had actually heard the plaintive meowing from the distant cottage or if she had just imagined it.

"Nalu!" she called out in dismay. "We forgot him!"

Miss Lilo heard her and started struggling to get out of the boat again.

"Nalu! Nalu!" she screamed as Mr. Manu held onto her. "Let me go!"

"I'll get him," Violet promised, dropping her plants in the boat and dashing back down the narrowing strip of sand. She heard Kai and Mr. Manu yell at her but kept racing as fast as she could.

Slipping back through the hole in the wall, she waded

down the length of the greenhouse, the waist-high water
slowing her to a crawl.

"Nalu!" Violet called. "I'm coming!"

She definitely didn't imagine the frantic sounds she heard
now. Pushing her way into the front room of the cottage,
she saw that the water was just at the top of the couch.
When Nalu saw her, he gathered himself and made a huge
leap across the room to Violet's waiting arms. She staggered
a bit as his weight hit her but held on tightly as she retraced
her steps through the greenhouse, clinging to the wet cat.
Nalu growled at her angrily, as if scolding her for forgetting
him in the first place.

By the time Violet made it back to the beach, there
was no beach left at all. The ocean was now crashing into
the base of the cliffs, and all three of her friends yelled for
Violet to run faster. She pushed her tired legs to give her
one last burst of energy. Tossing the surprised and angry cat
to Kai, Violet grabbed Mr. Manu's proffered hand, and he
yanked her into the boat. Within seconds they were revers-
ing away from the shore.

Violet sank to the floor of the boat at Miss Lilo's feet in
between the dozen or so potted plants they had been able to
save. Kai handed the hissing cat to her and moved to help
his dad. Relieved, Violet hugged the cat to her chest and felt
the cold fist of panic in her chest start to melt. She looked
up at Miss Lilo. Tears streamed down the old woman's
face as she watched the wild, storm-tossed ocean claim her
home. She clutched the bag full of seeds to her chest much
the same way Violet was clutching Nalu to hers.

"It's gone," Miss Lilo whispered in an agonized voice. "All of it, gone. All my work. All my plants. Everything is gone."

"No, it's not," Violet told her, reaching up to pat her knee. "We saved all these plants. And you got all those seeds. And more importantly, we saved you and Nalu."

Rain and tears mingling on her face, Miss Lilo looked down. "Oh, Nalu," she whimpered. At the sound of his name, Nalu struggled in Violet's arms until she released him and he could climb into Miss Lilo's lap. Once there he started purring determinedly. Miss Lilo dropped the bag of seeds and gathered the cat into her arms, burying her head in his wet fur and crying softly.

The ride back to the dock seemed to take forever as Mr. Manu skillfully battled the wind, rain, and waves to get them back safely. On the floor of the boat, Violet shivered uncontrollably, cold with shock and fatigue, even in the warm Hawaiian climate. Miss Lilo was gray with exhaustion, and even Kai showed signs of tiredness.

"Hold on," Mr. Manu told Violet as he helped her out of the boat. "You need some dry clothes and some food. We'll be back at the house soon."

Crowded with people and plants, the car made its way back up the cliffs. Violet fought to keep her eyes open and not fall asleep on the short drive, but the intoxicating smell of the *ola* flowers made her feel drowsy. Nalu didn't like the car at all and kept prowling back and forth from one window to another.

Miss Lilo, who had spent the drive absorbed in her own

thoughts, looked out the window and demanded, "Where are we going?"

"Back to the manor house," Mr. Manu told her.

"The manor house? No! I can't go there. Isn't there anywhere else we could go?"

"I'm sorry, but that's the safest place right now. We have to hurry: the hurricane is supposed to make landfall in about an hour." Mr. Manu's tone of voice left no room for argument, but Miss Lilo looked like she would rather jump out of the car.

"It will be OK," Violet told her reassuringly. "I'll be there to help. We can get your plants inside and make sure they are OK."

"My plants, right." She squared her shoulders as if preparing for battle. "I can do it for my plants. And my Nalu, of course. He needs to be inside."

"We're here," Mr. Manu announced as the car came to a stop.

Chapter 13

Everything about Miss Lilo radiated reluctance as they approached the front door, from her slow, dragging steps to her hunched, tense shoulders to her pinched expression. Violet matched her steps to the pace of the older woman, resisting the urge to hurry her in out of the rain.

The door opened as they approached, and Alula and Mrs. Manu dashed out into the rain, the relief clear on their faces as they hugged everyone.

"We were so worried you wouldn't get there in time!" Alula announced, shaking Violet in happy relief.

"Alula, Mrs. Manu, this is Miss Lilo." Violet made the introductions.

Mrs. Manu *tsked* her tongue impatiently. "You poor woman, let's get you out of the rain. There's plenty of time to talk later." She bustled them all inside and into the dining room, where the people seated at the table good-naturedly moved into the living room to make room for the newcomers. Soon Miss Lilo was settled in a chair with a warm mug in her hands. Violet's raincoat meowed as she sat down, and she unzipped it to allow Nalu to jump out. The soggy feline complained loudly for a moment before settling down to groom himself.

Violet noticed Miss Lilo studying the room and watched her eyes dart to the secret passage in the wall, and she couldn't tell if it was tears or rain on her wet face. Everyone was chattering in a friendly sort of way so that all Miss Lilo had to do was sit and sip and listen. Violet felt a surge of gratitude for Alula's mom, who seemed to know instinctively that Miss Lilo was uncomfortable. Burdened down with potted plants, Mr. Manu, Kai, and Lono entered the room.

"Miss Aka? Leilani?" Mr. Manu repeated when she didn't respond. She jerked in surprise and turned to look at him with wide eyes.

"Leilani?" she echoed faintly. "Yes, I suppose that is my name. I haven't heard it in years."

"Maybe you prefer Miss Lilo?" he asked kindly, and she nodded gratefully. "What should we do with your plants? Some of them look a little worse for the wear."

It was true. Many of the plants were damaged and drooping from their rough journey through the storm at the bottom of the boat. Miss Lilo jumped out of her seat, electrified with concern for her plants. Rushing to where they stood, she began examining each plant closely. Mrs. Manu whispered quietly to Alula in tones of disbelief, "They brought her *plants* with them?"

"I need to get to work. Some of these won't survive if I don't act fast," Miss Lilo announced with authority.

"Should we put them here on the table?" Kai asked.

"Yes—no, there's not enough room here. I need more room." Her brow furrowed in thought. As her eyes swept the room again, they paused once more on the secret passage. An idea lit up her face. "Of course, of course!" she cried out. "Everyone grab a plant and follow me."

Miss Lilo led the way out of the dining room, leaving Nalu in the company of Alula's twin brothers, who were feeding him scraps of their dinners. Heading back through the foyer and straight up the stairs, she walked confidently, although Violet was confused about why she would want to go upstairs. There was nothing up there except the bed-rooms and the office. But it was to the office that Miss Lilo led them, straight to the secret stairway behind the still-open bookshelf.

"Do you know how to open the secret door?" Alula gasped, toting a potted plant in each hand.

"Of course," Miss Lilo said matter-of-factly. "The secret is in the inscription."

Violet tilted her head in confusion. "The inscription on the bookshelf?"

Miss Lilo nodded and ran her fingers over the words. "*A'ohe hana nui ke alu'ia.* No task is too big when done together."

"But what does it mean?" Alula asked. The other members of her family, all carrying plants, crowded in to get a look at the inscription and to peer up the dark stairway.

"It means you need two people to open this door. Violet, did you find the knothole at the top of the stairs?"

Violet nodded. "Yes, but it doesn't do anything!"

"Did you find the one at the bottom of the stairs?" Miss Lilo showed them the matching knothole on the wall above the first step.

"We didn't even look down here!" Alula moaned dramatically. She pushed the knot, and just like the one at the top, the center popped inward. Everyone waited expectantly, but nothing happened. Miss Lilo smiled at Violet.

No task is too big when done together, Violet thought. *Done together.*

"You have to push them at the same time, don't you?" she asked and was rewarded with Miss Lilo's grin. Violet scampered up the stairs and found the now-familiar knothole.

"Ready?" she called down to Alula, who was standing ready to push the other knot. "One . . . two . . . three!"

This time when she pushed the knothole, she heard the groaning noise she was coming to associate with the opening of secret passages. Light filtered through as the door swung open, brightening the dim landing she was standing on. Dust motes hung thickly in the air.

"It's open!" Violet cried.

There was a scuffle at the bottom of the stairs as everyone except Miss Lilo tried to rush up at once and got stuck in the doorway. Alula pushed through first and raced up, followed by the rest of her family. Almost reluctantly, Miss Lilo followed one slow step at a time.

As the crowd reached the top of the stairs, Violet pushed the door completely open. A large room was revealed, with a sloping roofline just like Violet's attic bedroom. It was much brighter inside despite the dark storm clouds, thanks to the four large skylights in the sloped ceiling.

"Wow," Mr. Manu exclaimed, entering the room. "It's been decades since anyone's been here."

"What is this room?" Kai asked in confusion.

Three long tables ran down the center of the room, with a low desk along the far wall. Scientific equipment, covered in dust, sat silently on the desk, waiting to be used. Violet gently touched an expensive-looking microscope. Suddenly, the room was flooded with light. Miss Lilo stood at the doorway, her hand on the light switch.

"It's a lab, isn't it?" Violet asked.

Miss Lilo nodded. "Mr. Kahananui gave Makaio this room for his fifteenth birthday. We used to play up here, and eventually we used it to conduct our research." She walked forward and picked up an empty glass beaker. "This is where we discovered the formula to use the *ola* plant."

Shaking herself out of her memories, Miss Lilo gestured for everyone to bring their plants to the table farthest from the door. She hit another light switch, and a long grow light flickered to life above the table. Everyone carefully placed their plants under the lights and then stepped back.

"Violet, I need a spade and a pair of clippers. Oh, and an apron, of course. You can find them over there." She pointed in the general direction of a large cupboard.

Violet and Lono jumped into action, grabbing the supplies Miss Lilo had asked for.

"*Mahalo*, dears," Miss Lilo told them as she accepted the tools. Muttering to herself about not having any soil or fertilizers from her greenhouse, a sudden thought struck her. "The seeds!" Miss Lilo whirled around in a panic. "Where is my bag?"

"Here," Kai called out, unslinging the bulky bag from his shoulder and setting it on a table.

Heaving a sigh of relief, she unceremoniously dumped the hundreds of envelopes out on the long table. She looked between the pile of packets and the drooping plants anxiously.

"Can we help?" Alula asked.

Miss Lilo looked surprised—she was so used to having to do everything herself. "Yes," she replied gratefully. "I need to figure out if any of the seed packets got wet. They'll need to be spread out and dried."

"You leave that to us," Mrs. Manu told her, stepping up to the table. "You work on the plants, and we'll sort the seeds."

"*Mahalo*," Miss Lilo murmured fervently, moving back to the live plants. "Violet, you help me over here."

Alula, her parents, and her two brothers dug into the pile of seed packets. Violet set to work with Miss Lilo, following her instructions carefully as they tried to save the last few surviving *ola* plants. She counted the pots on the table.

Eleven.

Only eleven out of the two hundred or so that had been in the greenhouse. Her heart ached for Miss Lilo, who had lost her home today along with all of her plants. One tear slid down her face.

"It's OK," Miss Lilo said suddenly. Violet looked up to

find Miss Lilo looking right at her, as if she knew what she was thinking. "I started with only one plant, remember? Eleven is a blessing. And we saved so many seeds as well. Thanks to you, Violet. Without you, everything would have been lost."

Violet blushed and looked away, embarrassed but happy. Miss Lilo cleared her throat.

"All these plants are too wet. Go see if there is any newspaper on the desk; we can use that to absorb some of the excess water."

The desk was littered with dusty papers and one thick, yellowing envelope lying on top.

"Miss Lilo," Violet said slowly, "I think this is for you."

Miss Lilo didn't even look up. "I haven't been here for decades, Violet. I'm sure Makaio used the room after I left; anything left would be his."

"But it has your name on it," Violet insisted. She held the envelope up so everyone could see the words on the front.

For Lilo - Please read

Chapter 14

The rain beat with angry fists on the windows, and the wind howled around the manor house as the hurricane raged across the Big Island. But inside the hidden room, everyone was silent as Miss Lilo walked across the room and took the envelope. Her hand trembled as she read the words.

"Kaio," she whispered, equal amounts of bitterness and sadness in her voice. "It's his handwriting." Miss Lilo's knuckles whitened, and for one moment, Violet was afraid she intended to crush the letter.

"Give him a chance," she murmured gently. Miss Lilo glanced at her with a grimace but turned the letter over and ripped it open in one angry jerk. She pulled a stack of papers out and unfolded it. The first page was a short hand-written note.

Miss Lilo scanned it quickly. With a low gasp, she raised a shaking hand to her mouth in shock. She shuffled through the other papers in the stack.

"I don't believe it!" Miss Lilo repeated over and over.

Alula, never very patient, whispered excitedly, "What does it say?" and was promptly shushed by both of her parents. Miss Lilo handed Violet the letter, who read it out loud.

> *Lilo,*
>
> *I've sent you a dozen letters with no response. Knowing you, you probably burned them. You always were so stubborn, but maybe that's why we got along so well. The only person more stubborn than you is me! I would keep trying, but I'm running out of time. My doctors say I only have a few months left. It's cancer, just like Dad. Before I die I need to make things right.*
>
> *I plan to leave this letter in our secret lab. I hope when you are notified that I left the house to you, you will be curious enough to go and see the house, and you won't be able to resist visiting our lab. We had so many good times in that room, didn't we? Before I ruined everything.*
>
> *I want you to know that trading our friendship for money was the biggest mistake of my life. I have spent the last twenty years working to fix my error, and today I finally did it! I know you can't forgive me, but I hope this shows you how sorry I truly am. Go and change the world like we always planned.*
>
> *Your friend forever,*
> *Kaio*

Violet looked up. "I don't understand. What did he do?"

Miss Lilo held up the stack of papers. "It's our formula," she said through tears. "Makaio bought it back from the pharmaceutical company and then signed it over to me. This is all the legal paperwork. I own it now. He did that for me."

Behind her, Violet heard Lono whisper loudly, "Own what? What's going on?"

Her plants forgotten for the moment, Miss Lilo sank into a chair at the desk. She clutched the paperwork to her chest before laying it carefully on the desk and smoothing out the creases.

"All these years. I've owned the formula for ten years and never knew because I was too stubborn!" Miss Lilo hit her thigh with a fisted hand. "How could I have been so foolish?"

Violet patted her on the shoulder. "It's OK."

"No, Violet, it's not. Don't you see?" Her voice was strained. "If I hadn't been so angry, so full of bitterness, I might have opened Makaio's first letter ten years ago. Maybe I would have forgiven him and been able to see my best friend before he died. Maybe I would have moved out of my cottage with all my plants and research intact. Maybe I would be developing medicines from the *ola* flower and sharing them with the world. Instead, I spent all that time alone. Alone with nothing but my anger for company."

Silence filled the room. Violet struggled to find something to say. It was true that Miss Lilo's determination to hang on to her anger had led her to a life of loneliness. Her story was a sad one.

"We all make mistakes. Makaio made them, too," Violet began slowly, silently praying that God would help her find the right words. "Life is about second chances. About fixing our mistakes and trying again. As often as it takes. Makaio has given you a second chance to change the world. He wanted you to have it."

Miss Lilo brushed tears away from her eyes and chuckled ruefully. "He always liked to have the last word."

Everyone in the room laughed, breaking the tension. Miss Lilo stood up purposefully. "Well, it's never too late for a second chance, is it? I have to get started. There is so much to do. I have to save my plants so they can be replanted in the wild. Then I need to look into cultivating them commercially and figure out how to sustainably harvest the oils needed to make medicine." She clapped her hands together. "But first—did anyone find any newspaper?"

* * * * *

An hour later they descended from the hidden lab to the living room. The plants were tended to as best as possible, and the wet seeds were spread out to dry under the heat lamps.

Violet could tell that Miss Lilo was overwhelmed by the sheer number of people in the manor house after living alone for so long. Her eyes were wide and anxious, and she looked like she might bolt out into the storm at any moment.

"Why don't you come sit down, Miss Lilo?" Violet suggested and, matching actions to words, took her arm and

guided her to an isolated corner of the living room. Alula
trailed behind them, looking oddly determined. Once Miss
Lilo was seated in a tall armchair, Alula nudged Violet with
an elbow and gave her a significant look.

Violet took the hint. "Miss Lilo, this is my friend Alula
Manu. It was her father and brother who came with me to
rescue you."

Miss Lilo opened her mouth to reply, but Alula beat her
to it.

"*Aloha*, Miss Lilo, it's nice to finally meet you. Violet has
told me all about you. Your story is amazing! If it's all right
with you, I would like to write about it. You see, I'm going
to be a journalist," Alula rushed on in a single breath, as
if afraid that Miss Lilo would say no if she didn't get the
entire request out in one go. She pulled the battered flyer
out of her back pocket and handed it to Miss Lilo, who took
it automatically. "See, it's the Walton-Blue International
Writing Contest. They have prizes for different writing
projects, and I'm going to win the prize for the best article.
I've been looking for a good subject to write about, and I
think your story is it. So, what do you think? Please?"

Blinking at the sudden conclusion to Alula's speech,
Miss Lilo glanced at the paper in her hand but didn't say
anything. Alula looked confident as she waited, but Violet
could tell by the way she gripped her notebook that she was
nervous.

Looking directly at Alula, Miss Lilo asked bluntly,
"What is the prize?"

"One thousand dollars."

Miss Lilo's eyebrows shot into her hairline. "Really? And what are you going to do with a thousand dollars, may I ask?" Her voice was amused.

"Well, there are five kids in my family, and my parents can't afford to send us all to college." Alula shrugged. "I need to start saving money."

"You want to go to college?" Miss Lilo's face softened.

"Of course!" Alula said in such an earnest voice that no one could doubt her sincerity.

"And you want to write about me?"

Alula nodded.

Miss Lilo fell silent for a moment, deep in thought. The girls waited quietly while she considered the idea. Finally, she sighed heavily and shrugged.

"*A'a i ka hula, waiho i ka maka'u i ka hale,*" she murmured to herself, making Alula grin in excitement.

"What was that?" Violet asked.

"It's an old Hawaiian saying," Miss Lilo told her. "It means 'Dare to dance, leave shame at home.' It's time for me to dance. Let's do it, Alula."

Wasting no time, Alula pulled out her notebook, dragged a footstool up to Miss Lilo's chair, and, with her notebook perched on her knees and pen in hand, immediately launched into questions. Violet left them there, discussing details of Miss Lilo's childhood.

* * * * *

Afternoon faded into evening as Hurricane Tara crossed the Big Island, leaving a swath of downed trees and dropping

several inches of rain in just a few hours. Violet kept busy
inside the manor house, making sure everyone was comfortable and fed. She entertained the children when they started
to get bored and found blankets and pillows for the smallest
kids when they got sleepy. Later on she journaled about the
hurricane and sketched the various groups of people in the
house. From time to time, she took food to Alula and Miss
Lilo in their corner.

Late that evening, as the winds subsided, Violet's parents
finally made their way home. They came through the door
with a burst of rain, waking some of the children, and drew
the adults to the dining room to hear their story.

Snuggled under her mother's arm, Violet listened sleepily as her parents told everyone the good news. The storm
had turned and come up from the south, so the town had
escaped the flooding that had affected other, more exposed
parts of the island. Their homes and businesses were safe.

The house emptied quickly after that because most
people were anxious to get back to their homes. The Manu
family was the last to leave, with James and Emily fervently
thanking them for taking care of Violet. With the sleeping
twins in their parents' arms, the entire family finally left
around midnight. Alula had to be dragged away and only
left when Miss Lilo laughingly promised to talk to her
again the next day.

Miss Lilo took Mr. Manu's hand before he left and said
with sincere gratitude, "Thank you for rescuing me today.
I'm so sorry that my foolishness put you and your son and
Violet in danger."

Mr. Manu smiled tiredly, but sincerely. "It was my privilege."

Violet was thrilled to finally introduce Miss Lilo to her parents. She and Emily hit it off, especially after Emily insisted on seeing her lab upstairs and asked several pertinent questions about her research, one scientist to another. After learning that Miss Lilo's cottage had been destroyed by the high tide, James and Emily insisted that Miss Lilo stay with them in the guest room.

"I guess it's actually your guest room, isn't it?" James realized with a laugh.

Violet, who by now could barely keep her eyes open, told everyone good night and headed off to her attic bedroom. Before she got to the stairs, Miss Lilo called out after her.

"Violet?"

She paused with her foot on the first step. Miss Lilo hesitated. "Thank you for coming for me. Thank you for everything. If there is anything I can do for you . . ."

"Actually, there is something," Violet told her with a wide yawn.

Miss Lilo waited, one eyebrow raised.

"Tomorrow will you show me where the tunnel is?"

Chapter 15

Violet Thatcher stood on the edge of a volcano. Below her feet the land dropped away in steep walls down to the crater floor, where steam was billowing out of several vents. After the short walk from the car to the rim of the crater, Violet felt like she was steaming, too. The tropical sun blazed down on her head, and even the shorts and the light T-shirt she wore seemed much too warm for the Hawaiian climate. Violet tilted her face up and shoved her ball cap back on her head, trying to let the sea breeze cool her sweaty skin as she watched the steaming mouth of Kīlauea.

"She's beautiful, isn't she?" James Thatcher said happily. He was always happy standing on the edge of a volcano, although his eyes strayed from the view to the sulfur readings on his phone.

"Yeah, she is," Violet agreed, lifting her wildly curly hair up so the breeze could reach the back of her neck. "I can't believe we've already been here for three months."

Here at the Halemaʻumaʻu crater there wasn't much evidence of the devastation the latest eruption had caused. The

black river of freshly steaming lava was off to the east and not visible from the crater. The lava had hardened but not cooled completely in the ten weeks since the eruption. Here and there across the enormous crater floor, steam billowed up out of various cracks, but no lava glow was visible at the moment.

Violet had seen fourteen different volcanoes up close in her twelve years of life. Kīlauea was one of her favorites because it was possible to get so close to the crater, located as it was in Hawai'i Volcanoes National Park. On either side of Violet and her father, dozens of tourists feverishly snapped pictures of the volcano.

The wind suddenly shifted, and the cool sea breeze was replaced by a hot and humid current of air heated by its path across the crater floor, making Violet smile.

"Violet!"

They both turned to see Emily running up the path toward them, waving her hands above her head. Violet's breath caught in her throat. Was it time?

"Violet!" Emily came to a halt, breathing heavily, but managing to gasp out her message. "I got a call from Alula's mom. It's time!"

Violet squealed in excitement. Grabbing both her parents by the hand, she started dragging them toward the parking lot.

"C'mon, c'mon!" She urged her parents to go faster. "We have to hurry."

James and Emily exchanged grins but allowed Violet to tow them along. The car ride out of the park had never felt so long to Violet before. As they waited in the seemingly never-ending stream of cars, she bounced her knees impatiently.

"What if we're too late?" she moaned.

"Don't worry, pumpkin," her mother told her, watching her in the rearview mirror. "She said we have some time."

Finally, they got out of the park and picked up speed on the familiar road to the town. All the debris from the hurricane had been cleared away weeks ago, but large gaps in the forest still bore silent evidence of the storm's power. As they passed the turnoff to the manor house, Violet called out.

"Wait! What about Miss Lilo? She'll want to be there!"

"She's already there," Emily told her soothingly.

James drove straight to Alula's house, and Violet was out of the car before it came to a complete stop. Hurriedly, she headed straight for the beach, where a large group of people were gathered. It wasn't hard to find Alula in the crowd— she was jumping up and down and waving wildly.

"Are we too late?" Violet gasped.

"Nope! Right on time—come on, I saved you a spot." Alula seized her hand and led her to a gap in the crowd between Lono and Miss Lilo. Violet stepped into the gap and looked around. All the way down to the water, people were lined up in two rows, standing about six feet across from each other. Many of them were carrying flags, brooms, or umbrellas. Every face brimmed with excitement. The place Alula had saved was close to the water.

"The boil should happen any minute," Alula told her breathlessly, going up on tiptoes and peering up the beach.

"Why do they call it a boil?" Violet asked, but her words were lost in the sound of cheering from the top of the lines.

And then Violet got her answer because the pile of sand near the trees was moving! It appeared to be shifting and writhing, and suddenly dozens of baby turtles poured out of the nest, like water boiling over in a pot. Tiny sea turtles, no bigger than two or three inches long, scrabbled frantically in the sand, their small flippers propelling them forward, down toward the safety of the ocean.

A seagull let out a piercing screech above Violet's head. Hundreds of the seabirds were circling overhead, and she suddenly realized the purpose of the flags, brooms, and umbrellas. People swung them wildly in the air over the sea turtles, creating a corridor of safety for the babies and funneling them down to the sea. Following Alula's example, Violet jumped up and down and waved her arms to scare off the hungry birds. Even Miss Lilo, always so somber and reserved, yelled at the birds and waved a broom in the air.

Within minutes the baby turtles had reached Violet's position, and she studied the tiny creatures as they scurried past her. Their flippers, tails, and heads were dark black except where they were speckled with grains of white sand, but their shells were a beautiful golden brown and already detailed with intricate patterns. Violet marveled at the instinct that propelled them down the beach toward the best safety available—the clear blue water of the Pacific Ocean.

A loud cheer went up as the first hatchling reached the water and launched into the surf, only to be swept back up on the beach by the first wave. Undaunted, it continued crawling toward the sea and finally achieved deeper water and swam gracefully away. Tears ran down Violet's face as the river of baby turtles streamed by until each one was swimming away. The entire process had taken less than twenty minutes. The crowd finally spread out along the shore and watched as the last baby turtle disappeared.

Everyone in the crowd wandered away, leaving Violet, her parents, Miss Lilo, and Alula alone on the beach. Mr. Manu joined them and clapped a hand on Violet's shoulder.

"Eighty-nine!" He exclaimed. "Eighty-nine of the eggs hatched. We only lost three eggs when moving the nest. Eighty-nine new *honuʻea* and all thanks to you, Violet!"

Violet blushed. "I'm just glad they hatched before I left. I almost missed it."

Alula looked at her, instantly understanding. "You're going? Your parents got their next assignment?"

Violet nodded. "We're leaving tomorrow for Iceland."

"Iceland? Wow—that's great," Alula said, a little glumly. An uncomfortable silence fell over the group until Mr. Manu spoke up.

"We're having a luau at the house to celebrate the hatching. We'd better head over before the boys eat all the food."

Alula was uncharacteristically quiet on the walk back. As they approached the small yellow house, Lono burst out the door, waving a large yellow envelope above his head.

"Alula! It came! It finally came!" He shoved the envelope into her hands, and everyone could clearly see the name on the return address label: Walton-Blue International Writing Contest.

All the color drained out of Alula's face, and her hands shook as she looked at the envelope. Bewildered, she asked, "What do I do?"

"Open it!" Violet told her, grinning at her normally confident friend. Lono patted her on the back, clearly impatient to know what was inside the letter.

"But, what if—what if—" Alula stuttered.

Miss Lilo stepped up next to her young friend. "Don't let a 'what if' stop you from living, my dear," she advised gently.

Alula closed her eyes for a second, took a deep breath, and then carefully opened the envelope. She tilted it, and the contents fell into her hand: a glossy magazine, a white letter, and a long, thin check for one thousand dollars.

Alula studied the check in shock. "We did it?" She looked up at Miss Lilo's beaming face. "We did it!"

"You did it, Alula. You did it," Miss Lilo told her triumphantly.

Alula opened the magazine, and everyone leaned in to see the headline. The words "How Falling Off a Cliff Helped One Girl End a Fifty-Year Feud" were blazoned across the top. A picture of Miss Lilo and Violet standing in front of the manor house, holding a potted *ola* flower, dominated the front page.

"Alula, you're amazing!" Violet told her, pulling her into a tight hug. "I knew you could do it."

* * * * *

The luau turned into a real party. Everyone wanted to celebrate the successful hatching, everyone wanted to congratulate Alula and read her published article, and everyone wanted a chance to say goodbye to the Thatchers. The party lasted for hours as the Hawaiian sun set in the sky until it was a burning ball of fire sinking into the ocean. Torches were brought out, pounded into the sand, and lit so that the fun could continue. The kalua pork, wrapped in leaves and cooked in a pit on the beach, was the most delicious thing Violet had ever tasted. Alula even tried to teach Violet the hula, although both girls couldn't stop laughing at her efforts. Mrs. Manu sang a sad song in Hawaiian while Kai played along on the ukulele.

Eventually, though, it was time for the Thatchers to leave. They still needed to pack for their flight the next morning. Miss Lilo had no plans to rent the house out again once they left because she would live there from now on. In the last ten weeks, she had already brought the gardens back to life with Hawaiian plants of every kind, including her precious *ola* plants. She spent her days busily and cheerfully re-creating from memory the research she had lost in the storm.

Violet went searching for Alula to say goodbye and found her friend on the porch of the house with a book and a *lei* in her hands.

"So . . . Iceland, huh?" Alula asked her.

"Yeah."

"How many volcanoes are there in Iceland?" Alula asked with a hint of a teasing smile.

Violet opened her mouth but then paused. "You know what? I have no idea!"

"Then my work here is done," Alula exulted. Without another word she draped the flower necklace, made from plumeria blossoms, around Violet's neck. She knew they were Violet's favorite. Then she placed the book in her hands. The solid blue cover was blank. Violet opened it and discovered that the pages were also blank.

"It's for you, Violet. To write and illustrate your own story." Alula placed a battered and creased flyer on top of the book. "The next round of submissions for the contest is due in three months. I know you've thought about it. If I can do it, then so can you. I can't wait to read your story."

Violet's eyes brimmed with tears as she hugged her friend. "Thank you, Alula. Thank you for everything. Goodbye."

Alula shook her head and touched the *lei* around Violet's neck. "Nuh-uh. *Aloha*."

"*Aloha*."

In the dark back seat of the car, Violet listened to her parents discuss their new assignment in Iceland. She hugged the empty book to her chest, her mind full of possibilities and dreams, and looked out at the ocean as they drove back to the manor house for the last time.

1.0NSP469-159880 Printed in USA Feb-2025